I0427176

# Make Money with Peer to Peer Lending

## Guide to Peer to Peer Lending Investments for Financial Growth

### Harper Wells

Life Level Up Books, LLC

**Make Money with Peer-to-Peer Lending:** Guide to Peer-to-Peer Lending Investments for Financial Growth

Copyright © 2023 by Harper Wells

Disclaimer Notice:

Please note the information contained within this document is for educational and entertainment purposes only. All effort has been executed to present accurate, up to date, reliable, complete information. No warranties of any kind are declared or implied. Readers acknowledge that the author is not engaged in the rendering of legal, financial, medical or professional advice. The content within this book has been derived from various sources. Please consult a licensed professional before attempting any techniques outlined in this book.

By reading this document, the reader agrees that under no circumstances is the author responsible for any losses, direct or indirect, that are incurred as a result of the use of the information contained within this document, including, but not limited to, errors, omissions, or inaccuracies.

This book is written for entertainment purposes only. The statements made in this book do not necessarily reflect the present market at the time of reading or current views of the author. Furthermore, the author accepts no responsibility for actions taken by the reader as a result of information presented in this book.

# MAKE MONEY WITH PEER TO PEER LENDING

# Contents

1. Lend Your Way to Wealth     1

2. The Basics of Lending and Earning     4

3. Building a Winning Strategy     20

4. Risk Management     27

5. Understanding and Leveraging Borrower Profiles     34

6. Legal and Ethical Considerations     41

7. Technology in Lending     50

8. Scaling Your Lending Business     58

9. Personal Finance and Lending     67

10. Global Lending Trends and Opportunities     77

11. The Future of Lending and Earning     86

12. Conclusion     95

# Chapter 1
# Lend Your Way to Wealth

F inancial independence isn't just a fleeting aspiration but a tangible goal, "Make Money with Peer-to-Peer Lending" emerges as a guiding light, illuminating the intricate pathways of modern lending and earning. This book isn't merely about grasping the mechanics of lending; it's about transforming your financial landscape, turning every challenge into a stepping stone towards success.

The realm of lending has evolved remarkably, influenced by technology, market trends, and shifting consumer behavior. "Lend & Earn" dives into this evolution, offering a clear, concise blueprint of the landscape. Here, you'll not only learn about the various aspects of lending but also how to align them with your personal financial goals. It's about crafting a strategy that resonates with your financial vision, whether you're taking initial steps or seeking to enhance your approach.

As we traverse the complex world of risk and reward, "Make Money with Peer-to-Peer Lending" stands as a trustworthy guide. Balancing risk isn't just a matter of crunching numbers; it's a psychological exploration. This book illuminates strategies to mitigate risks, aiding you in understanding your risk profile and making informed decisions that align with your financial ambitions.

Beyond risk management, the book takes a comprehensive look at understanding and leveraging borrower profiles. It's not just about whom you lend to; it's about grasping their needs, behaviors, and how these factors influence your lending decisions. Effective communication with borrowers isn't merely a skill; it's a crucial instrument in forging lasting relationships that are mutually beneficial.

But this expedition isn't just about relationships and strategies. "Lend & Earn" also focuses on the critical aspects of legal and ethical considerations in lending. The terrain of lending is continuously reshaped by legal frameworks and ethical practices. This book guides you through these complex aspects, ensuring that your lending practices are not only profitable but sustainable and responsible.

Technology plays a pivotal role in modern lending, and "Make Money with Peer-to-Peer Lending" embraces this topic fully. From the rise of fintech to the integration of AI and big data in lending decisions, the book explores how technology can revolutionize your lending practices, enhancing efficiency and borrower experience.

As we progress towards the later chapters, the focus shifts to growth and scalability. Expanding a lending business requires a unique mindset, one that balances ambition with stability. This book provides insights into effective marketing strategies, the power of partnerships, and how to navigate the realm of collaborative ventures.

"Lend & Earn" also brings personal finance into the mix, showcasing lending as a viable component in your financial arsenal. It offers a fresh perspective on integrating lending into your financial plan, balancing traditional investments with lending activities.

The exploration culminates with a global perspective, exploring international lending markets and emerging trends. The future of lending is dynamic, shaped by technological advancements and regulatory changes. "Lend & Earn" prepares you for this future, equipping you with the knowledge and strategies to thrive in the evolving world of lending and earning.

It's evident that "Make Money with Peer-to-Peer Lending" is more than just a guide; it's a pathway to financial empowerment. It encourages you to think, reflect, and act, transforming your financial path into a story of success and fulfillment. Informed, strategic, and ethical lending – a world where your financial dreams are not just possible but within reach.

# Chapter 2
# The Basics of Lending and Earning

E ver find yourself gazing at your bank statement, wondering if there's a secret manual for adulting that you somehow missed? Fear not, my financially perplexed friend, for we're about to embark on a rollercoaster ride through the riveting world of lending and earning. Forget the snooze-fest you associate with finance – it's time to transform your financial understanding from "What's a credit score?" to "I got this, money!"

**Unlocking the Financial Matrix:** In a world where compound interest feels like a mystical force determined to rob you of your avocado toast dreams, understanding the basics of lending and earning is the golden ticket. It's the Rosetta Stone of personal finance – a language that, once decoded, opens doors to a realm where your money isn't just surviving; it's thriving.

**Clearing the Jargon Jungle:** First things first, let's clear the air of financial jargon. No one wants to feel like they need a Ph.D. in economics just to grasp the ABCs of lending and earning. So, buckle up as we navigate away from the jargon jungle and head straight for the oasis of financial clarity. Consider finance as a foreign country – you wouldn't walk in without a basic guidebook, right? Well, consider this your crash course in 'Financese.'

**The Power of the Plastic:** Credit cards, those deceptive little rectangles that seem harmless until they're not. It's like inviting a Tasmanian devil into your wallet – thrilling at first, but the aftermath is chaotic. So, let's demystify the plastic puzzle: Pay your balance in full each month. It's like training your credit card to sit and roll over, but instead of treats, you earn a stellar credit score. Interest rates are the frenemies of finance. Keep them low, and your financial well-being will thank you later.

**The Savvy Art of Borrowing:** Lending isn't just for billionaires and Bond villains. We've all been there – needing a financial lifeline when life throws a curveball. But let's be smarter about it. Ditch the payday loans. They're like the frenemies you call in a crisis but regret as soon as the dust settles. Personal loans can be your financial fairy godmother if used wisely. Just remember, moderation is the key.

**Earning Without Selling a Kidney:** Now, onto the earning side of the equation. If you're tired of living paycheck to paycheck, it's time to upgrade your earning potential. Side hustles are the rockstars of the financial world. Whether it's dog walking, freelancing, or selling hand-knit scarves on Etsy, find your money-making jam. Investments aren't just for the Wolf of Wall Street. Start small, diversify, and watch your money grow like a well-nurtured garden.

As we navigate the money maze, remember this isn't about becoming the next Warren Buffett overnight. It's about mastering the basics, building a solid foundation, and inching closer to financial freedom.

Reflect on your spending habits. Are you splurging on things that bring you joy or drowning in buyer's remorse? It's time for a financial reality check.

In this world of financial complexity, think of your newfound knowledge as a GPS, guiding you through the twists and turns of lending and earning. It's not about perfection but progress. So, dear reader, are you ready to transform your financial understanding, from bewildered bystander to the maestro of your money orchestra? The baton is in your hands; it's time to conduct your financial symphony.

## Riding the Wave: Navigating the Landscape of Modern Lending

Financial landscapes shift like sand, and understanding the evolution of lending practices is the key to financial empowerment. Exploring the evolution of lending practices can provide insights into the roots of contemporary lending.

**Evolution of Lending Practices:** Lending isn't a static practice; it has morphed over centuries, responding to societal, economic, and technological shifts. To comprehend the present, we must unravel the threads of the past. Explore the evolution of lending from the early barter systems to the sophisticated financial instruments of today. As we examine history, you'll gain insights into the roots of contemporary lending practices.

**Key Market Trends in Lending:** The financial world is a dynamic ecosystem, and to thrive, you need to ride the currents of market trends. We'll dissect the latest shifts in lending – from the rise of peer-to-peer lending to the impact of global events on interest rates. This step is your compass to understanding the market forces that shape the availability and terms of loans.

**Embracing the Digital Frontier:** In the era of smartphones and artificial intelligence, technology is the linchpin of modern lending. Dive into the digital tools reshaping the lending landscape, from online applications to algorithmic credit scoring. We'll demystify the technology behind lending platforms, empowering you to navigate the digital frontier with confidence.

**Steering Clear of Pitfalls:** Armed with historical context, market insights, and technological understanding, it's time to dive into practical advice. Learn how to prepare a robust loan application, optimize your credit score, and negotiate favorable terms. But, beware the hidden reefs – we'll guide you through potential problems like predatory lending practices and the pitfalls of excessive debt.

Ever wondered how your credit score impacts your ability to secure a loan? Or questioned the role of algorithms in determining your creditworthiness? We'll unravel these mysteries and address common concerns, ensuring you're equipped to navigate the lending landscape with confidence.

As we conclude this exploration of the landscape of modern lending, remember: financial empowerment is not a destination; it's a continuous path. Armed with historical insights, market awareness, and technological literacy, you're well-prepared to make informed financial decisions. The waves of change will keep rolling, but now you have the skills to ride them with finesse. So, go forth, navigate the lending landscape, and shape your financial destiny.

## Navigating Your Lending Odyssey: A Millennial's Guide to Financial Freedom

Embark on a quest to unlock the secrets of financial empowerment! In this guide, we'll unravel the complexities of lending, exploring the path to your financial goals. Whether you dream of owning your first home, launching a business, or simply aim to understand the lending landscape, this guide serves as your compass to navigate the financial seas and plot a course to success.

### Identifying Your Lending Goals

Let's set sail by defining your destination. What are your lending goals? Are you eyeing a mortgage for your dream home, funding your education, or perhaps diving into the world of small business loans? Take a moment to record your aspirations; it's the roadmap to your financial success.

Understanding your goals is the North Star guiding your lending path. Consider the purpose, duration, and amount needed. Are you in it for the long haul or a short-term venture? Knowing this helps tailor your lending strategy to fit your unique needs.

Ever found yourself daydreaming about that cozy house or your passion project? Your lending goals are the keys to turning those dreams into reality.

### Assessing Your Financial Readiness

Ahoy, sailors! Now that we know our destination, let's inspect the ship. Assessing your financial readiness is like checking the sails, ensuring they're robust enough to weather the lending storm.

Dive into your financial sea and examine your credit score, income stability, and debt-to-income ratio. A strong ship (financial health) ensures smoother sailing when negotiating with lenders.

Ever been caught in a storm without an umbrella? Assessing your financial readiness is your financial umbrella, ensuring you're prepared for the unexpected.

### Choosing the Right Lending Platform

Land ho! As we approach the lending shores, the choice of platform becomes crucial. Will you row your own boat or join a fleet? Choosing the right lending platform can be the wind in your sails or the anchor holding you back.

Explore traditional banks, credit unions, and online lending platforms. Each has its merits and drawbacks. Research diligently, comparing interest rates, terms, and customer reviews. Your choice should align with your goals and financial readiness.

Choosing a lending platform is like selecting the crew for your voyage. Make sure they share your vision and won't jump ship when the seas get rough.

Don't be swayed by flashy offers. Look beyond the surface, ensuring the platform's values align with yours.

Watch out for hidden fees or predatory lending practices. It's the hidden rocks beneath the surface that can sink your financial ship.

As we conclude our expedition through the lending seas, remember that this is just the beginning. Your lending odyssey is a personal quest, and with each step, you are charting your course to financial freedom.

No clichés, no empty promises—just a roadmap to guide you. Now, armed with the knowledge of your lending goals, financial readiness, and the right platform, set sail confidently into the vast ocean of financial possibilities.

May your lending path be prosperous, and your financial sails catch the winds of success. Bon voyage, financial trailblazers!

## Mastering Risk: Navigating the Perilous Seas of Finance

In the vast ocean of financial possibilities, navigating the turbulent waters of risks and rewards is both an art and a science. In this guide, we'll unravel the secrets of balancing risk and return, explore strategies for risk mitigation, and explore the psychology of risk in lending. So, tighten your seatbelt; we're setting sail into uncharted territories!

**Understanding the Risk-Return Tradeoff:** Every financial decision involves a delicate dance between risk and return. Think of it as a seesaw – the higher the potential return, the greater the risk. But fear not, as we unveil the art of finding that sweet spot. To start, consider your risk tolerance, financial goals, and the time horizon of your investments. By striking the right balance, you can optimize returns while weathering the occasional storm.

**Strategies for Risk Mitigation:** Now that you're acquainted with the seesaw of risk and return, let's arm you with strategies to mitigate the downsides. Diversification is your trusty shield, spreading your investments across different assets to minimize the impact of a single setback. Additionally, keep a keen eye on market trends and stay informed – knowledge is your best ally in navigating the unpredictable currents of finance.

**The Psychology of Risk in Lending:** As we dive into the psychology of risk, it's crucial to understand the intricate dance between lenders and borrowers. Lenders assess risk through a meticulous lens, considering factors like credit history, debt-to-income ratio, and the purpose of the loan. On the flip side, borrowers must be aware of the psychological biases influencing their decisions. Are you prone to optimism bias or overconfidence? Recognizing these tendencies empowers you to make sound financial choices.

Now that we've outlined the steps, let's sprinkle in some practical advice. When diversifying your portfolio, resist the urge to overcomplicate – simplicity is often the key to success. Stay vigilant against the allure of high-risk investments promising quick gains; they might be sirens leading you astray. And remember, the psychology of risk isn't just about numbers – it's about understanding your emotions and making decisions with a clear head.

Ever felt the rush of excitement and fear when making a financial decision? You're not alone. Navigating risks and rewards is an emotional rollercoaster for everyone. Have you ever wondered why some people are risk-averse while others embrace it? Understanding these dynamics unlocks the door to financial wisdom.

As we dock our financial ship, armed with newfound knowledge, remember that mastering risk is an ongoing voyage. The seas may be unpredictable, but armed with the right strategies and insights, you're well-equipped to navigate them. This guide has been your compass, helping you understand the delicate balance between risk and return, unveiling strategies to mitigate risks, and shedding light on the psychology of lending.

So, fellow adventurers, may your financial venture be prosperous and your risks well-managed. As you set sail into the vast expanse of financial possibilities, remember: the greatest rewards often lie just beyond the horizon of calculated risks. Bon voyage!

## LendingClub

Navigating the financial world can often feel like trying to solve a Rubik's Cube—complex, frustrating, and with a dose of colorful chaos. Enter LendingClub, a peer-to-peer lending platform that turns traditional banking on its head by connecting borrowers directly with investors. For young adults dipping their toes into the pool of personal finance, understanding the nuances of such a platform can be your lifebuoy. Let's demystify LendingClub, revealing not only its shiny perks but also the slippery spots you'll want to sidestep.

## The Bright Side of LendingClub

**Accessibility and Convenience:** Unlike your traditional brick-and-mortar banks, LendingClub operates entirely online. This means you can apply for a loan in your pajamas at 2 AM—because who really keeps banker's hours? The platform offers personal loans, business loans, and auto refinancing, among other services, making it a one-stop shop for many of your financial needs.

**Competitive Interest Rates:** LendingClub often provides rates that are more palatable than those offered by conventional banks, especially if you have a good credit score. It's like getting a VIP pass at a concert but for loans.

**Peer-to-Peer Charm:** The concept of borrowing from real people, not faceless institutions, adds a human element to the process. You might be financed by someone who understands exactly why you need that car repair or small business boost.

## The Other Side of the Coin

**Risk of Higher Interest Rates:** If your credit score has seen better days, you could end up with interest rates that soar high enough to give you vertigo. LendingClub uses a risk assessment model that might not always work in your favor.

**Fees, Fees, Fees:** Origination fees can take a bite out of your loan before you even see the funds. Make sure to read the fine print as if it's the secret to eternal youth, so you aren't caught off guard.

**Limited Direct Communication:** Since transactions are conducted online, getting help or clarification might take longer than expected. Imagine emailing a brick wall and waiting for it to email back. Sometimes, it can feel a bit like that.

## Tips for Success with LendingClub

1. **Know Your Numbers:** Understand your credit score and financial situation inside and out. It's less about navel-gazing and more about financial self-awareness. This knowledge will empower you to negotiate better terms or choose the right time to apply for a loan.

2. **Comparison Is Key:** Always compare LendingClub's offers with other financial products. It's like dating—don't settle for the first one that comes along without seeing what else is out there.

3. **Read the Reviews:** Just as you wouldn't eat at a restaurant with only one star, don't skip the user reviews for Lending-Club. They can provide insights into real user experiences, highlighting potential red flags or green lights.

4. **Plan for Repayment:** Before you even apply, have a clear plan for repayment. Budgeting isn't just for control freaks; it's for anyone who doesn't want to be blindsided by their financial choices.

By treating LendingClub not as a magic bullet but as a tool that requires careful handling, you can leverage its benefits while avoiding common pitfalls. The platform offers a modern twist to lending, reflecting a shift towards more democratized financial services. Yet, it demands a savvy user who will approach the process with a critical eye and a well-prepared mind.

Reflect on how these tools fit into your broader financial picture. Consider how adopting or rejecting this modern lending method impacts your financial health and aligns with your personal values. By integrating new technologies thoughtfully, you ensure they serve you rather than overwhelm you.

# Prosper

Imagine stepping into a marketplace where instead of fruit and trinkets, the stalls are lined with opportunities to grow your money or get that much-needed loan. Welcome to Prosper, a pioneer in the peer-to-peer lending arena, offering a different flavor to the financial mix than platforms like LendingClub. In a world brimming with financial options, understanding how Prosper stands out can be your compass to navigating this bustling market.

## Why Choose Prosper?

**Diverse Loan Purposes:** Prosper is not just about consolidating debt (though it's great for that too); it's also about funding your next big adventure or home improvement project. The flexibility in loan purposes makes it akin to having a Swiss Army knife in your financial toolkit.

**Straightforward Terms and Conditions:** Prosper prides itself on transparency. The terms are laid out with all the finesse of a well-played piano, clear, crisp, and straightforward to follow.

**Investor Attraction:** With Prosper, investors can choose individual loans to invest in or set criteria for automatic investments, making it highly appealing for those looking to directly impact someone else's story while adding a chapter to their investment saga.

## Points to Consider

**Higher Qualifications for Borrowers:** Prosper might give you the side-eye if your credit isn't up to scratch. With a minimum credit score requirement that's typically higher than some competitors, it's like a bouncer at a club, ensuring only the 'right' profiles get through.

**Potentially Steeper Fees:** Just when you thought you were running through the daisies, Prosper might hand you a bill for origination fees that feels like a bouquet of nettles. These fees are percentage-based, so the more you borrow, the more you might pay.

**Less Forgiveness on Late Payments:** Miss a payment and Prosper might not be so... prosperous for your financial health. The platform can be stricter about late payments, adding fees and penalties that could make your wallet wince.

## How Does Prosper Compare?

While both Prosper and LendingClub dance to the tune of peer-to-peer lending, there are nuances in their choreography. For instance, Prosper typically requires a higher credit score for entry, positioning itself as a bit more exclusive, akin to a high-end club versus a popular downtown bar. LendingClub, meanwhile, offers a wider range of loan products and might be more forgiving for those with less-than-perfect credit.

## Navigating Success on Prosper

1. **Check Your Credit First:** Before you apply, know your credit score like you know your favorite movie line. This will save you from the plot twist of being rejected.

2. **Shop Around:** Compare rates and terms on Prosper with other platforms. You wouldn't buy the first car you test drive without checking out a few others, right?

3. **Understand the Fees:** Read the fine print as if it's a detective novel. Knowing all the possible fees can help you calculate the true cost of your loan.

4. **Be Timely:** If you choose Prosper, set reminders for payments. Late fees are real, and they can stack up like a bad habit.

Prosper offers a modern approach to lending and investing that merits consideration. Its stricter credit score requirements and fee structure are pivotal points to ponder when choosing a platform. By exploring Prosper with a critical eye, you can harness its potential to meet your financial needs and perhaps even enhance your investing journey.

## Upstart

In a digital age where algorithms dictate everything from our playlists to our pizza toppings, why not let them help with our financial decisions too? Enter Upstart, a lending platform that uses artificial intelligence to shake up the traditional credit system. Upstart isn't just another name in the game; it's redefining the rules, making it crucial for the tech-savvy and financially curious to understand what sets it apart from the likes of Prosper and LendingClub.

### The Upside of Upstart

**AI-Driven Decisions:** Upstart leverages sophisticated algorithms and machine learning to assess borrower risk, which goes beyond just looking at credit scores. This means even if your credit history is more 'abstract art' than 'impeccable portrait,' you might still qualify for a loan.

**Higher Approval Odds:** Because of its unique approach to credit assessment, Upstart boasts higher approval rates compared to traditional models. It's like having a benevolent guardian angel who sees your potential rather than just your past financial flubs.

**Speedy Service:** Upstart's application process is streamlined and efficient, often delivering loan decisions in minutes and funding loans as quickly as one business day post-approval. For anyone who's ever waited in a bank line wondering if they'll be there until retirement, Upstart's speed is a breath of fresh air.

## The Downside of Upstart

**Potentially High Interest Rates:** Despite the innovative credit model, Upstart's loans can come with steep interest rates, especially for those with less-than-stellar credit. It's like a high-speed train to your destination that might cost you as much as a flight.

**Origination Fees:** Upstart charges origination fees, which can range up to 8% of the loan amount. This fee is deducted from the loan before you even see the money, so you might end up with less cash than you counted on.

**Limited Loan Uses:** Unlike Prosper, which allows loans for a wide variety of purposes, Upstart's loans are somewhat more restricted, primarily focusing on debt consolidation, credit card refinancing, and personal expenses.

## Upstart vs. Prosper and LendingClub

When comparing Upstart to platforms like Prosper and LendingClub, the standout difference is its use of AI in the credit evaluation process. This not only opens the door to applicants with varied financial backgrounds but also speeds up the approval process dramatically. While Prosper and LendingClub rely more heavily on traditional credit score metrics, Upstart's model allows for a broader interpretation of creditworthiness.

## Tips for Navigating Upstart Successfully

1. **Understand Your Credit Profile:** Even though Upstart is lenient, knowing your credit score and history is crucial. Awareness of your financial standing will help you anticipate loan terms more accurately.

2. **Evaluate the Full Cost:** Factor in interest rates and origination fees to determine the total cost of the loan. Just like planning a vacation, it's not just about getting there; it's about affording the whole trip comfortably.

3. **Read Reviews and Testimonials:** See what previous borrowers have to say. Their experiences can offer valuable insights and help you set realistic expectations.

4. **Plan for Repayment:** Ensure that you have a solid repayment plan in place. Upstart may be quick to loan you money, but remember, it's not a gift. It's a financial responsibility that needs careful handling.

Upstart's novel approach to lending using AI makes it an intriguing option for those who might be overlooked by traditional banks. Its methodology not only broadens access to credit but also aligns with a more digital, fast-paced world where traditional metrics might not tell the whole story.

Reflect on how integrating AI-driven financial solutions like Upstart into your financial strategy could enhance your economic flexibility and resilience. In the evolving narrative of personal finance, platforms like Upstart play a crucial role in illustrating that technology can be a powerful ally in achieving financial health and empowerment.

# Chapter 3
# Building a Winning Strategy

I n the grand theater of life, where the spotlight often shines on the innovators and disruptors, you might be wondering, "How the heck do I build a winning strategy that propels me to success without drowning in the sea of clichés and business jargon?" Fear not, fellow road warrior, for we're about to embark on a quest that transcends the mundane and catapults you into the realm of lending legends.

Now, let's cut the fluff and dive into the nitty-gritty of crafting a strategy that doesn't just break the mold but obliterates it. Hold on to your calculators because we're about to revolutionize the way you think about lending success.

**Dare to be Different:** Forget what your business professor told you about playing it safe. In the world of lending, the safe route is a one-way ticket to mediocrity. Embrace the unconventional, dance with risk (but don't French kiss it), and watch as your lending strategy evolves from mundane to mind-blowing. As the great Warren Buffett once said, "Risk comes from not knowing what you're doing." So, get to know your lending game inside out, and let the risk become your strategic dance partner.

**The X-Factor: Relationships Matter More Than Rates:** In a world obsessed with interest rates, be the maverick who understands that lending success isn't just about numbers. It's about forging genuine connections. Build relationships that outlast market fluctuations and economic downturns. People are not just credit scores; they're human beings with dreams, fears, and the occasional penchant for late-night ice cream binges. Be the lender who sees beyond the FICO score and into the soul of the borrower.

**Break Free from Spreadsheet Shackles:** Let's be real; spreadsheets are like the beige wallpaper of the lending world – functional but oh-so-dull. Break free from the monotony of endless cells and embrace technology that not only streamlines your lending process but also adds a dash of pizzazz. Envision a lending world where algorithms do the heavy lifting, and you, my friend, get to focus on the art of strategic brilliance. It's not just lending; it's lending 2.0, where innovation meets interest rates.

**Fail Fast, Succeed Faster:** Contrary to popular belief, failure isn't the Voldemort of business; it's Dumbledore, whispering invaluable lessons in your ear. Embrace failure, learn from it, and use it as fuel for your path to lending stardom. Remember, every successful entrepreneur has a closet full of failures – consider it your rite of passage.

**The Crystal Ball Strategy: Anticipate, Don't React:** Predicting the future might be reserved for mystics and fortune tellers, but in lending, you can come pretty darn close. Anticipate market trends, consumer behaviors, and economic shifts like a financial Nostradamus. Be the lender who doesn't react but rather orchestrates the symphony of lending success with a well-timed baton.

In the grand tapestry of lending success, your strategy is the warp and weft weaving the threads of innovation, relationship-building, and foresight. So, as you go on this path of strategic enlightenment, remember this: In the lending game, the only limits are the ones you impose on yourself.

As the ink dries on this chapter, take a moment to reflect on your own lending odyssey. Are you ready to break free from the shackles of conventional wisdom and pave your road to lending success? The adventure begins not with the first step but with the audacity to take it. Happy lending, fearless strategist!

## Your Financial Future: Understanding and Achieving Your Goals

Embark on the path to financial empowerment! In this guide, let's explore the pivotal steps to understanding your financial goals, aligning lending activities, and setting realistic expectations. Ever felt lost in a sea of financial jargon and conflicting advice? It's time to cut through the noise and get to the heart of the matter. By the end of this exploration, you'll be equipped with the tools to make informed decisions, ensuring your financial experience is not just a process but a purposeful one.

**Clarifying Your Financial Objectives:** Have you ever found yourself navigating through the complexities of personal finance, trying to articulate your aspirations? It's time to cut through the noise and get to the heart of the matter. Take a moment to reflect on your financial goals, both short-term and long-term. Create a clear vision of what financial success looks like for you. Whether it's buying a home, starting a business, or retiring comfortably, defining your goals is the first step toward achieving them.

Practical Advice:

- Create a list of your financial goals.

- Prioritize them based on urgency and importance.

- Be specific and realistic about the timelines for each goal.

**Aligning Lending Activities with Goals:** Now that your goals are crystal clear, it's time to ensure your lending activities are working in harmony with your objectives. Whether it's a mortgage, student loan, or credit card debt, every financial commitment should serve a purpose. Evaluate your existing loans and determine if they align with your goals. Refinancing or restructuring might be necessary to optimize your financial strategy.

Practical Advice:

- Review all outstanding loans and their interest rates.

- Explore opportunities to consolidate or refinance for better terms.

- Consider consulting with a financial advisor for personalized guidance.

**Setting Realistic Expectations:** In a world of instant gratification, it's crucial to set realistic expectations for your financial adventure. Understand that building wealth takes time, and setbacks are a natural part of the process. Avoid the allure of quick fixes and focus on sustainable strategies. Embrace the path, learn from challenges, and celebrate small victories along the way.

Practical Advice:

- Develop a budget that aligns with your goals.

- Build an emergency fund to weather unexpected financial

storms.

- Educate yourself on investment options and risks.

Remember, this path is not about perfection but progress. Continuously reassess your goals, adapt to changes, and stay committed to your financial well-being. As you navigate the dynamic landscape of personal finance, embrace the lessons, and enjoy the empowerment that comes with understanding and achieving your financial goals. Your future self will thank you.

## Lending Opportunities: A Guide to Smart Choices

The realm of financial decisions can shape your future. In this guide, we'll embark on a path together, exploring the art of choosing the right lending opportunities. Whether you're a seasoned investor or just dipping your toes into the finance pool, understanding the nuances of evaluating lending options is a skill that will serve you well.

**Recognizing the Landscape:** Understanding lending opportunities starts with recognizing the diverse landscape they present. From traditional banks to online platforms, options abound. Each comes with its own set of pros and cons. Consider your financial goals and risk tolerance when surveying the lending landscape.

**The Power of Due Diligence:** Now that we see the terrain, it's time to put on our detective hats. Due diligence is your secret weapon. Investigate interest rates, terms, and hidden fees. Don't be afraid to ask questions – this is your financial future we're talking about. Look beyond the shiny numbers; the devil is often in the details.

**Leveraging Expert Insights:** Expertise is invaluable. Seek advice from financial gurus, and tap into the collective wisdom of those who've been there, done that. Online forums, podcasts, and even a chat with your neighborhood financial whiz can provide insights you might have overlooked. Learning from the experiences of others can be a shortcut to financial wisdom.

Armed with knowledge, it's time to address potential pitfalls. Watch out for predatory lenders and unrealistic promises. If a deal seems too good to be true, it probably is. Protect yourself by being skeptical and asking questions. Trust your instincts; they're often your best guide.

**Engaging with Your Financial Future:** We've covered a lot, but now it's time to put your newfound knowledge into action. Engage with your financial future – negotiate terms, explore alternatives, and don't be afraid to walk away from a deal that doesn't align with your goals. Your financial future is in your hands – make decisions that resonate with your values.

You've just graduated from Lending Opportunities 101. As you navigate this financial landscape, remember that choosing the right lending opportunity is not just a transaction; it's a strategic move that can shape your financial destiny. Stay informed, be diligent, and always trust your instincts. The path to financial success is yours to conquer. Happy investing!

## Mastering Wealth: A Strategic Guide to Resource Allocation

In the realm of financial uncertainties, understanding how to effectively allocate your resources can be the key to unlocking a prosperous future. We're not dreaming; we're exploring a strategic reality waiting for you to embrace.

**Balancing Your Portfolio:** Achieving financial success is like creating a masterpiece. Each stroke matters, and so does each investment in your portfolio. Diversification is the brushstroke, spread your investments across different assets to minimize risk. Keep an eye on the canvas, regularly reassess your portfolio to ensure it aligns with your goals.

**Timing and Market Considerations:** Timing the market is an art, not a guessing game. Let's paint a clearer picture. Patiently wait for the right moment: Avoid impulsive decisions; patience is a virtue in investing.

Embrace market trends: Recognize and adapt to market movements without succumbing to panic.

According to renowned financial analysts, maintaining a balanced portfolio and strategic market timing are key elements of successful wealth management. It's not a speculative claim but a well-researched fact.

As you navigate the field of wealth, remember:

Regularly review your portfolio and adjust it to align with your financial goals.

Potential problem: Emotional investing can lead to hasty decisions; stay rational and focused on your long-term objectives.

Have you ever felt the rush of making impulsive decisions in the market? We've all been there. Let's learn together how patience and strategy can triumph over the roller coaster of emotions that is financial management.

As we conclude our exploration into the realm of strategic resource allocation, remember: wealth is not a destination but a process. Each decision, each calculated move, contributes to the masterpiece of your financial success. Embrace the knowledge, apply the strategies, and watch your wealth flourish. This isn't just about numbers; it's about sculpting a future where financial freedom is your masterpiece.

# Chapter 4
# Risk
# Management

In the vast expanse of business uncertainties, the hunter doesn't merely survive; they thrive. Mastering risk management isn't just a strategy; it's your ticket to turning uncertainty into your strategic advantage. And no, I won't bore you with the typical corporate drivel or throw around buzzwords that could lull even the most caffeinated entrepreneur to sleep. Let's embark on a jaunt that's equal parts wisdom and wit, and trust me, you won't need a business dictionary to navigate it.

**Embrace the Chaos, Unleash the Beast:** You're on a roller coaster hurtling through the labyrinth of unpredictability. Sounds fun, right? Now, envision you're not just a passenger; you're the one steering this wild ride. Risk management is your roadmap, your GPS through this chaotic thrill ride. Embrace the chaos, and you'll find that within the uncertainty lies your entrepreneurial beast waiting to be unleashed.

**The Fortune Favors the Bold Myth:** Ever heard the saying, "Fortune favors the bold"? Well, let's dissect this little piece of conventional wisdom. Boldness alone won't cut it. It's like saying a diet of ice cream will get you that summer body. Boldness needs a sidekick, and that sidekick is calculated risk. Don't just be audacious; be strategic. Dive into risks armed with data, insights, and a touch of daring. That's the winning combo that'll have fortune knocking at your door.

**Risk Isn't a Four-Letter Word:** Contrary to popular belief, risk isn't a four-letter word whispered in hushed tones at corporate gatherings. It's the unsung hero of innovation. Take a leap, make a move, and watch your comfort zone shrink in the rearview mirror. Sure, it's nerve-wracking, but hey, so is public speaking, and people do that voluntarily. Risks are the spice of entrepreneurial life, and it's time to make your business a flavorful feast.

**The Tightrope Walker's Guide to Decision-Making:** Ever seen a tightrope walker tiptoeing between skyscrapers? Now, visualize that wire is your decision-making process. Every step is a delicate dance between risk and reward. But here's the secret: it's not about eliminating risk; it's about perfecting the art of balance. Embrace the wobbles, adjust your weight, and soon you'll be striding confidently between the tallest challenges.

**The Crystal Ball Is a Myth:** Now, let's address the elephant in the room—predicting the future. Spoiler alert: the crystal ball is a myth. If it existed, we'd all be lottery winners. Instead, we're left with a barrage of unknowns. But fear not, intrepid entrepreneur! You don't need a crystal ball; you need scenario planning. Anticipate the twists and turns, and you won't just navigate uncertainty; you'll dance with it.

**The Real MVPs: Feedback Loops:** If risk management had an MVP, it would be feedback loops. Visualize driving without course correction; you'd end up in a ditch. Your business is no different. Create feedback loops that keep you on track. Listen, learn, and adjust. It's the secret sauce that turns good risk management into a symphony of strategic brilliance.

As we wrap up this roller coaster ride through the jungle of risk management, remember this: uncertainty isn't the enemy; it's your canvas. Mastering risk management isn't about avoiding the unknown; it's about dancing with it. So, tighten your shoelaces, entrepreneur, because where the brave roam free, that's where the true adventure begins. In the wild, unpredictable terrain of business, those who master risk don't just survive; they triumph.

## The Labyrinth: Identifying and Mitigating Lending Risks

Embark on the exploration of lending, where opportunities abound, but so do risks. In this guide, we'll unravel the intricacies of identifying potential risks in lending. Think of this as your map through the labyrinth, guiding you to navigate the twists and turns with confidence. By the end, you'll not only be able to identify the various types of lending risks but also spot early signs of risk exposure, understand risk profiling, and fortify your lending strategy against potential pitfalls.

**Types of Lending Risks:** Consider lending risks as puzzle pieces. We'll explore credit risk, market risk, and operational risk, ensuring you can identify them in your lending endeavors. Think of this as your risk identification toolkit.

**Early Signs of Risk Exposure:** Just like a detective scans a crime scene, we'll teach you to scrutinize financial landscapes for anomalies. From unexpected spikes in default rates to subtle shifts in market trends – consider these your breadcrumbs to potential risks.

**Risk Profiling:** Now, let's craft your risk profile. It's like creating a superhero character sheet, but for your lending strategy. We'll dive into risk tolerance, risk appetite, and risk capacity, ensuring your lending decisions align with your risk profile.

According to financial experts like Warren Buffett and Ray Dalio, a thorough understanding of risks is crucial for any successful investor or lender. Their wisdom, combined with extensive research, forms the backbone of the insights shared in this guide.

In the world of lending, forewarned is forearmed. Watch out for common pitfalls like over-reliance on credit ratings and failure to adapt to market shifts. Stay vigilant, and you'll be well-prepared to navigate the complexities.

Have you ever felt that pit in your stomach when something doesn't quite add up? This guide is your compass to navigate those uneasy feelings, transforming uncertainty into confidence.

And there you have it – your guide to identifying and mitigating lending risks. As you step out into the lending landscape armed with this knowledge, remember: risks may be inevitable, but with the right insights, you're well-prepared to turn challenges into triumphs. Happy lending!

## Mastering Risk: Ways to Secure Future

In the unpredictable landscape of life, understanding how to navigate risk is like holding the keys to a secure future. Whether you're a budding entrepreneur or a seasoned investor, the ability to mitigate risks is a skill that transcends industries. In this guide, we'll dive into three essential pillars of risk management: tools for mitigation, diversification strategies, and legal safeguards. By the end, you'll be equipped with a toolkit that not only shields you from potential pitfalls but propels you toward success.

### Tools for Mitigating Risk

**Identify and Assess Risks:** Risks can be elusive, lurking in the shadows until they strike. Begin by conducting a thorough risk assessment. What are the potential threats to your venture or investment? Once identified, assess their likelihood and impact.

**Risk Mitigation Tools:** Armed with a clear understanding of your risks, it's time to deploy mitigation tools. From insurance policies tailored to your industry to risk modeling software, leverage these tools to create a robust defense against uncertainties.

**The Power of Early Detection:** Consider the story of Sarah, an entrepreneur who implemented advanced analytics to foresee market trends. By identifying potential risks early on, she navigated through stormy economic waters and steered her business to prosperity.

### Diversifying to Reduce Exposure

**The Power of Diversification:** Diversifying your portfolio is a tried-and-true strategy for risk reduction. Spread your investments across various sectors or asset classes to avoid overreliance on a single source of income.

**The Art of Portfolio Diversification:** Meet Alex, an investor who diversified his investments across stocks, bonds, and real estate. When the stock market faced a downturn, his real estate investments acted as a buffer, minimizing losses and preserving his wealth.

**Reassess Regularly:** Diversification is not a one-time event; it's an ongoing process. Regularly reassess your portfolio and adjust your strategy based on changing market conditions and your financial goals.

### Legal Safeguards

**Importance of Legal Protections:** Legal safeguards act as the backbone of risk management. Contracts, trademarks, and compliance measures provide a solid foundation, shielding you from legal entanglements.

**Consult with Legal Experts:** Don't navigate the legal landscape alone. Seek guidance from legal experts who specialize in your industry. Their insights can help you craft airtight contracts and ensure compliance with ever-evolving regulations.

**The Price of Ignorance:** Let's examine the cautionary tale of James, who neglected legal safeguards in his business. Facing a lawsuit due to contractual ambiguities, he learned the hard way that a stitch in time saves nine.

As we wrap up about the risk mitigation, remember that understanding and implementing these strategies is an ongoing process. The world is dynamic, and risks evolve. Continuously educate yourself, stay informed about industry trends, and adapt your risk management strategies accordingly. By doing so, you'll not only shield yourself from potential pitfalls but also position yourself for success in an ever-changing world. Mastering risk is not just a skill—it's a mindset that propels you toward a future of security and prosperity.

## Decoding Risk: Advanced Strategies for Informed Decision-Making

Embarking on the path of advanced risk management is like navigating uncharted waters. But fear not, for the benefits are immense - a heightened ability to foresee, understand, and navigate potential pitfalls in both personal and professional realms. In this guide, we dive into the heart of risk management, exploring data-driven decision-making, predictive analysis, and the power of a proactive approach.

**Unveiling the Power of Data:** Understand how to collect, interpret, and leverage data to make informed decisions. Think of data as the stars guiding your ship. In the era of information, data is your North Star. Collect it, interpret it, and let it illuminate your path. In your personal and professional life, data isn't just numbers; it's the story waiting to be told.

**Predictive Analysis:** Learn the art of predictive analysis, foreseeing potential risks and opportunities. It's like having a telescope to spot storms before they hit. Predictive analysis is your crystal ball, allowing you to anticipate challenges and opportunities. Like a seasoned sailor predicting a storm, you'll foresee disruptions and steer your ship with confidence.

**Embracing Proactivity:** Adopt a proactive mindset to anticipate and mitigate risks. It's about setting sail with purpose, not merely reacting to the waves.

In risk management, being proactive is your anchor. Anticipate challenges, plan ahead, and embrace the thrill of navigating the seas rather than being tossed by the waves.

In the unpredictable waters of risk, you need a seasoned sailor's advice:

- Trust your data but verify its sources.

- Embrace uncertainty; it's where opportunities hide.

- Cultivate adaptability; rigid sails break in the storm.

You, at the helm of your ship, confidently navigate the unpredictable tides. Isn't that a dream? We're not just managing risk; we're conquering it.

As our voyage concludes, remember this isn't a final destination but a newfound skill set. Risk management is a lifelong experience, and you're now equipped to navigate its intricacies. So, set sail, explore the uncharted, and may your seas be ever calm. Bon voyage!

# Chapter 5
# Understanding and Leveraging Borrower Profiles

I n the labyrinth of finance, understanding borrower profiles is the X-factor. Forget the cookie-cutter advice you've been fed. It's time to unwrap the mystery behind leveraging borrower profiles and unlocking the true potential of client relationships. We're not here for the same old dance; we're here to disrupt the narrative and shake up your preconceptions about what makes a borrower tick.

In this dynamic exploration, you're not just dealing with numbers; you're unraveling stories. Every borrower profile is a novella waiting to be deciphered. It's a tale of dreams, challenges, and a quest for financial freedom. Ditch the monotony of conventional wisdom; let's break into the realms of understanding borrower profiles like never before.

**Borrower Profiles: Beyond the Numbers:** It's easy to see a credit score as a red or green light. But hold on—life isn't a traffic signal. People aren't two-dimensional beings defined by numerical judgments.

Their stories are complex, woven with the threads of experiences, ambitions, and setbacks. So, why reduce them to a mere FICO score? Look beyond the credit score. Understand the narrative—why a borrower's score took a hit and how they've triumphed over challenges.

**The Myth of One-Size-Fits-All Strategies:** You've probably been told there's a golden formula for borrower engagement. Spoiler alert: It's a myth. Your approach can't be a one-size-fits-all, like that superhero costume you regretted wearing on Halloween. Borrowers are unique individuals with distinct needs and aspirations. It's time to customize your strategy accordingly. Tailor your approach based on individual borrower profiles. Personalization isn't just a buzzword; it's the secret sauce for lasting relationships.

**Unmasking the Feedback Loop:** Ever heard of the feedback loop? It's not just a concept reserved for tech wizards. Borrowers exist within a perpetual loop of experiences and reactions. The way you engage with them influences their financial behavior, creating a loop that can either lead to success or spiral into chaos. The power is in your hands. Understand the borrower's feedback loop. Your actions today shape their financial decisions tomorrow.

**The Human Touch in a Digital World:** In a world drowning in algorithms, don't forget the human touch. Your borrowers aren't robots; they're humans with emotions, fears, and aspirations. Inject empathy into your interactions. A little understanding can go a long way in forging relationships that withstand the test of time. Don't underestimate the power of empathy. It's not just good for borrowers; it's great for your business.

**From Borrower Profiles to Success Stories:** Here's the golden nugget: Every borrower profile is a potential success story. Your role is to be the catalyst. Move away from the notion of merely providing loans; become the architect of financial success. Help your borrowers rewrite their narratives and transform challenges into triumphs.

In the realm of borrower profiles, it's not just about analyzing data; it's about deciphering the human experience. Break free from the shackles of conventional wisdom, challenge the norms, and be the pioneer who transforms borrower profiles into success stories. Because when you understand the intricacies of your clients, you don't just lend money; you invest in futures. And that's a game-changer.

## Borrower's Blueprint: A Deep Dive into Borrower Data Analysis

In the vast landscape of finance, one key to unlocking success lies in deciphering the intricacies of borrower data. Visualize having a roadmap that not only guides your decisions but empowers you to navigate the twists and turns of financial transactions with confidence. That's precisely what understanding borrower data offers. In this guide, we'll dive into the importance of borrower analysis, explore key metrics for borrower assessment, and discover how to wield borrower data effectively.

### Recognizing the Importance of Borrower Analysis

To grasp the significance of borrower analysis, we must first understand its role as the cornerstone of financial decision-making. Borrower analysis is not a mere formality; it's the telescope through which we observe the financial universe. By scrutinizing borrower data, we gain insights into creditworthiness, risk levels, and repayment patterns. This knowledge, is like a seasoned captain navigating treacherous waters, empowers us to make informed lending decisions.

Have you ever wondered why some financial ventures flourish while others flounder? Borrower analysis holds the answer.

### Key Metrics for Borrower Assessment

Navigating the sea of borrower data requires a compass calibrated to key metrics. Think of these metrics as stars guiding your financial ship. Credit scores, debt-to-income ratios, and payment history emerge as beacons illuminating the borrower's financial voyage. Understanding these metrics isn't just about deciphering numbers; it's about unraveling the borrower's financial story.

When assessing credit scores, consider not only the number but also the factors influencing it. A holistic approach unveils a more comprehensive borrower profile.

### Utilizing Borrower Data Effectively

Armed with a profound understanding of borrower data and equipped with key metrics, the next frontier is effective utilization. This step involves transforming raw data into actionable insights. Just as a skilled sculptor shapes raw material into a masterpiece, effective utilization of borrower data molds financial decisions that stand the test of time.

Beware of over-reliance on automated algorithms. While they streamline processes, a nuanced human touch remains crucial for interpreting subtle nuances in borrower data.

Remember that borrower analysis is not a static art but a dynamic science. It evolves, adapts, and thrives on the nuances of human financial behavior. Armed with the knowledge of borrower analysis, you possess a formidable tool that transcends numbers and charts. It's the compass guiding you through the financial terrain, ensuring your decisions are not just data-driven but wisdom-infused.

In your financial adventure, let borrower analysis be your North Star. Illuminate the path with knowledge, navigate the challenges with insight, and witness the flourishing of your financial endeavors.

## The Borrower Personas: Crafting Personalized Lending Experiences

Understanding your borrowers is like holding the key to a treasure chest. Personalized lending approaches that resonate with your borrowers' needs and behaviors. Sounds like a dream, right? Well, get ready to turn that dream into a reality. In this guide, we'll dive into the art of building borrower personas, demystifying the process of creating detailed profiles that will revolutionize the way you approach lending.

**Understanding Your Audience:** Borrowers aren't just numbers; they're real people with dreams, fears, and habits. Understanding them is your superpower. Dive into demographics, conduct surveys, and get cozy with social media analytics. The more you know, the better you can tailor your lending approach.

Ever wonder why your friend prefers e-books over paperbacks? It's the same with borrowers—knowing their preferences is the key to connection.

**Creating Detailed Borrower Profiles:** Details matter. The more you know about your borrowers, the more personalized and effective your lending strategies become. Don your detective hat and gather intel—financial history, spending habits, and even personal interests. This is the canvas for your borrower portrait.

Ever notice how Netflix suggests the perfect show? That's because they know you inside out. Visualize doing the same for your borrowers.

**Understanding Borrower Needs and Behaviors:** Needs change, behaviors evolve. Staying in sync helps you anticipate, adapt, and offer solutions before they're even sought. Regular check-ins, feedback loops, and keeping an eye on market trends. It's like predicting the weather—only it's financial clouds and sunshine.

Think about the last time someone surprised you with exactly what you needed. That's the feeling borrowers get when you anticipate their needs.

As you embark on a borrower persona, here's a nugget: patience pays off. Expect road bumps. Maybe your initial profiles won't hit the bullseye. But iterate, refine, and watch the magic happen.

Now, think about you're at a crossroads, wondering which path to take. Borrowers face the same dilemma. Be the guide they didn't know they needed.

Now, as we wrap up into the heart of borrower personas, remember: this isn't about ticking boxes or meeting quotas. It's about weaving a tapestry of trust, understanding, and financial symbiosis. So, here's to lending not just with numbers but with heart. Because, in the end, it's not just about lending—it's about connecting.

## Borrower Communication: Unlocking Trust and Success

In finance and lending, effective communication with borrowers is not just a skill; it's the cornerstone of success. Visualize navigating the lending landscape with the confidence to handle any conversation, build trust effortlessly, and turn challenging situations into opportunities. This guide is your key to mastering the art of borrower communication, providing techniques that transcend the mundane and elevate your interactions to new heights.

**Understanding Techniques for Effective Communication:** Communication is an art, and as with any art form, there are techniques that can be mastered. Explore the nuances of active listening, clarity in messaging, and the power of empathy. Each technique is a brushstroke on the canvas of effective borrower communication.

**Building Trust and Rapport:** Trust is the currency of any lending relationship. Dive into strategies that go beyond mere transactions. Learn how to build authentic connections, foster transparency, and cultivate a borrower's confidence. Trust is not given; it's earned, and this section will show you how.

**Handling Difficult Conversations with Grace:** Difficult conversations are inevitable, but they don't have to be daunting. Discover proven strategies to navigate sensitive topics, manage emotions, and turn challenges into opportunities. From overdue payments to unexpected financial hardships, you'll be equipped to handle it all with finesse.

Have you ever wondered how the power of a well-timed question can transform a conversation? Dive into each step and find rhetorical questions that resonate with your own experiences. Recognize the common concerns within borrower communication and embark on a path of self-discovery.

As we wrap up this exploration of effective borrower communication, remember that these techniques are not just tools; they're your keys to unlocking success. The lending landscape is ever-changing, but with the skills acquired here, you're equipped to thrive. Continue refining your approach, stay engaged with your borrowers, and watch as your communication becomes a catalyst for lasting success.

# Chapter 6
# Legal and Ethical Considerations

I n the vast, complex landscape of finance, there's a less-traveled path intertwining ethical considerations with lending practices, leading to sustainable success. In this world, profit doesn't come at the expense of morality; loans aren't ticking time bombs, and the act of borrowing isn't a Faustian bargain. This is the realm of ethical lending, where financial success and moral integrity coexist like the yin and yang of personal and professional growth.

Now, let's be real for a moment. In a world where "business as usual" often means compromising ethics for profit, ethical lending might sound like a unicorn in a field of thoroughbreds. But bear with me, fellow seekers of financial enlightenment, for this isn't a utopian dream. It's a paradigm shift waiting to happen—one that can reshape the way we view lending, borrowing, and financial success.

Let's cut through the jargon and the smoke screens; ethical lending isn't about sipping organic green tea while discussing interest rates in a room filled with ethereal light. It's about injecting fairness into a system that has often preyed on the vulnerable. It's about recognizing that profit isn't the villain, but the means to a virtuous end. It's about flipping the script on traditional lending and creating a win-win scenario where lenders profit, borrowers thrive, and the moral compass points firmly north.

Think of it this way: traditional lending is like a one-night stand—quick, transactional, and often regrettable. You get what you want (or need) momentarily, but the aftermath is a haze of interest rates, hidden fees, and the lingering question, "Was it worth it?" Ethical lending, on the other hand, is a long-term relationship. It's about mutual respect, transparency, and ensuring that both parties walk away satisfied. It's the difference between a fleeting moment and a lasting connection.

Now, let's address the elephant in the room—interest rates. The very mention of them can send shivers down the spine, like a nails on a chalkboard or a cat video interrupted by an ad. But here's the deal: ethical lending isn't about eliminating interest; it's about making it fair. It's about creating interest rates that don't make you question your life choices. Think of interest rates as spices in a dish. Too much, and it's inedible; just right, and it's a culinary masterpiece. Ethical lending aims for that Goldilocks zone where everyone gets a satisfying taste without burning their tongues.

Now, I'm not here to sugarcoat the challenges. Transitioning to ethical lending means challenging the status quo, and change is never a walk in the park. It's more like a sprint through a labyrinth filled with bureaucratic hurdles and skeptical glances. But here's the secret sauce: small steps lead to significant strides. Start by questioning the norm. Challenge the idea that profit must come at the expense of integrity. Let's redefine success as a harmonious blend of financial prosperity and ethical backbone.

In the words of Mahatma Gandhi, "Be the change that you wish to see in the world." The world of ethical lending isn't a distant dream—it's a reality waiting for pioneers. As we navigate this uncharted territory, let's remember that the process is as important as the destination. Ethical lending isn't just about the numbers; it's about the stories, the people, and the impact we leave on the financial landscape.

So, fellow adventurers in the realm of financial wisdom, let's embark on this path together. Let's challenge the norm, question the status quo, and redefine success on our terms. In a world where ethical lending isn't just a buzzword but a way of life, sustainable success isn't a myth—it's the destination we're carving with every ethical loan, fair interest rate, and transparent transaction. The compass is in our hands, and the path is ours to shape. Here's to ethical lending, sustainable success, and a financial landscape where everyone wins. Cheers to a future where unicorns roam freely and ethical lending isn't an exception but the rule.

## Legal Landscapes: Navigating Lending Principles and Regulatory Realms

The legal framework in lending is where the twists and turns of legislation can either be a boon or a bane for businesses and individuals alike. In this guide, we'll unravel the complexities surrounding key legal principles, help you navigate regulatory environments, and show you how to stay ahead of the curve with the ever-evolving legal landscape. Understanding this terrain isn't just a matter of compliance; it's your key to unlocking opportunities and safeguarding your financial endeavors.

**Decoding Legal Lingo:** Visualize legal terms as a foreign language – we'll be your translators. From APR to default, we'll break down the acronyms and phrases so you can speak the language of lenders.

**Navigating Regulatory Waters:** It's a sea out there, and regulations are the currents. We'll help you set sail without getting lost in compliance. From Dodd-Frank to GDPR, we've got your regulatory compass.

**Staying in the Know:** The legal landscape is like a garden; it keeps growing. We'll show you how to tend to it – subscribing to updates, attending webinars, and staying connected to legal communities. Because being in the dark is so last season.

### Practical Advice on Potential Problems

- Legal Lingo Life Hacks: Ever heard of the 'Plain English' movement? We'll teach you how to spot the loopholes and understand the fine print. No more nodding along in confusion.

- Regulatory Sailing Tips: Create a compliance calendar. Think of it as your financial planner for regulations. We'll guide you on how to set reminders, so you're never caught off guard.

- Staying Updated Wisdom: Join legal forums and discussion groups. It's like having your own army of legal advisors. We'll share our top picks, so you're always in the loop.

Ever felt lost in the jungle of legal documents? We hear you. Throughout this process, we'll ask questions that probably echo your thoughts – no more feeling like you're in this alone.

As we wrap up, remember, the legal landscape isn't a static painting; it's a dynamic masterpiece. By understanding the legal principles in lending, navigating regulatory environments, and staying updated, you're not just compliant – you're a maestro conducting your financial symphony. Now, go out there and conquer the legal jungle like the savvy navigator you are.

## Ethical Lending Mastery: Navigating Profit and Responsibility for Business Success

Ethical lending mastery is where profit and responsibility dance in harmony, propelling businesses toward unprecedented success. In this guide, we'll unravel the intricacies of ethical lending practices, exploring their definition, dissecting their impact on business success, and delving into the delicate art of balancing profit with responsibility. Brace yourself for a path that transcends the mundane, as we unveil the secrets to navigating the complex landscape of lending with ethics as your guiding star.

### Defining Ethical Lending

**Understanding the Core:** Let's grasp the essence of ethical lending. It's more than a buzzword—it's a commitment to fairness, transparency, and accountability. Think of it as the North Star guiding your financial decisions, ensuring that each lending practice aligns with values that go beyond mere profit.

Ask yourself, "Does this decision contribute positively to the community, environment, or society at large?". Remember, to beware of the temptation to cut corners for quick gains; ethical lending demands a meticulous approach.

**Impact of Ethics on Business Success:** Now, let's explore how ethical lending isn't just a moral choice; it's a strategic one. A business built on ethical foundations enjoys the trust of stakeholders, fostering long-term relationships that transcend economic downturns.

Ever wondered why customers stick with certain brands? It's the trust factor. Ethical lending builds trust, creating a loyal customer base.

According to a Harvard Business Review study, companies with a strong commitment to ethical practices outperform their counterparts in the long run.

**The Art of Equilibrium:** The challenge lies in achieving equilibrium between profit and responsibility. Striking this balance requires a nuanced approach, like a tightrope walking.

Think about the profit and responsibility as scales; adjusting one side impacts the other. The key is to find the sweet spot where both coexist harmoniously. Be reminded to regularly reassess your lending practices, adapting them to evolving ethical standards and market dynamics.

Remember that embracing ethical principles isn't a sacrifice; it's an investment. The returns, measured in trust, sustainability, and long-term success, far outweigh the fleeting gains of unethical practices.

In your pursuit of ethical lending, let your compass be guided not solely by profit margins but by the impact your decisions have on the world. As the architect of your business destiny, let ethics be the cornerstone, building a legacy that transcends mere financial success.

Navigate the lending landscape with wisdom, empathy, and a commitment to leaving a positive mark on the world. The league of ethical lending masters—where prosperity and responsibility walk hand in hand toward a brighter future.

## Compliance and Documentation: Streamlining Processes and Navigating Legal Landmines

Demystify the intricacies of essential documents, automate compliance processes, and adeptly handle legal disputes. By the end, you'll not only have a newfound understanding but also practical tools to ensure your business sails smoothly through the seas of regulations.

### Understanding Essential Documents and Compliance

- **The Power of Documentation:** In the grand theater of business, documentation plays the lead role. Visualize it as the script that guides your every move. Contracts, policies, and records are your supporting actors, ensuring a seamless performance. But why the spotlight on documentation? It's not just about bureaucracy; it's about clarity, protection, and a roadmap for success.

- **Clear Contracts for Smooth Sailing:** Crafting ironclad contracts is an art. Dive into the nuances of language, stipulations, and contingencies. Think of it as your business's insurance policy, shielding you from unforeseen storms.

- **Policies: Your North Star:** Policies aren't just rulebooks; they are your moral compass. Unveil the secrets of creating policies that align with your values, ensuring ethical business practices that resonate with your team and clients.

### Automating Compliance Processes

- **Embracing Automation:** Now, let's fast forward to the future – a realm where compliance isn't a tedious manual task but a well-oiled machine humming in the background. Automation is the key, and it's not just for tech gurus. We'll guide you through the steps to effortlessly integrate automation into your compliance processes.

- **Choosing the Right Tools:** Not all automation tools are created equal. Discover the gems that fit your business like a glove. From document management to compliance tracking, we've got you covered.

- **Streamlining Workflows:** Ever wished compliance could be a background process? Streamlining workflows is the answer. Learn how to optimize your operations for efficiency without compromising on compliance.

### Handling Legal Disputes

- **Ninja Moves for Legal Disputes:** Legal disputes are the ninjas of the business world – silent, deadly, and waiting to strike. But fear not; armed with knowledge, you can turn the tide in your favor. Let's dive into the martial arts of dispute resolution.

- **Negotiation Strategies:** Negotiation isn't about winning or losing; it's about finding common ground. Uncover proven strategies to navigate negotiations and emerge victorious without burning bridges.

- **The Art of Mediation:** When disputes escalate, mediation is your secret weapon. Learn the art of compromise, facilitated by a neutral third party. It's not surrender; it's a strategic move towards resolution.

As we reach the summit of our exploration, reflect on the invaluable insights gathered. Picture a business landscape where compliance is not a burden but a catalyst for growth. Essential documents, automated processes, and adept dispute resolution – the trinity that propels your business into the future.

Develop a personalized action plan based on the gems you've un-covered. Implement changes gradually, ensuring a seamless transition to a compliance powerhouse.

In the ever-evolving world of business, the learning never stops. Stay informed, adapt to changes, and keep refining your compliance strategies.

As the curtains fall on our path through compliance and documentation, remember – this isn't just a guide; it's your roadmap to resilience. Navigate the legal labyrinth with confidence, armed with essential documents, automated processes, and dispute resolution mastery. Your business isn't just surviving; it's thriving in the face of challenges. So, embrace the knowledge, empower your endeavors, and let compliance be the wind beneath your wings. Onward to success!

# Chapter 7
# Technology in Lending

In the electrifying realm of lending, where tradition meets the digital age, a pulsating heartbeat of innovation awaits, poised to transform your lending practices. Buckle up, because we're about to embark on a wild ride where technology isn't just a tool; it's the secret sauce to revolutionize the way you lend and borrow. Move over, conventional wisdom; there's a new sheriff in town, and its name is Tech-tastic Lending.

Seated comfortably on your couch, smartphone in hand, envision securing a loan without navigating the labyrinth of paperwork. No more sweating over credit scores like it's your high school GPA. Thanks to cutting-edge algorithms, the future of lending is bright, breezy, and beautifully uncomplicated. And hey, who said financial transactions can't be as smooth as a perfectly crafted cappuccino?

Hold your horses; we're not just talking about streamlining the borrowing process. Technology is here to sprinkle some magic dust on the entire lending landscape, from the dusty old bank vaults to the hip fintech startups. We're breaking barriers, my friend, and redefining the very essence of lending.

Now, before you skeptics roll your eyes and mutter about the good ol' days of face-to-face transactions, consider this: technology isn't robbing lending of its humanity; it's infusing it with efficiency and accessibility. Envision lending becoming so user-friendly that your grandma could navigate it with a cup of chamomile tea in hand. Yes, even Grandma can be a fintech guru.

Let's debunk the myth that technology in lending is a cold, heartless machine. In reality, it's the compassionate sidekick you never knew you needed. Think of it as a financial superhero, swooping in to save the day when traditional lending methods would leave you stranded on a financial cliff.

"But what about the personal touch?" you might ask. Fear not, for technology is like a personal finance wizard, tailoring solutions to your needs faster than you can say, "Is this interest rate for real?" It's not just about algorithms; it's about a financial GPS guiding you through the maze of options, ensuring you emerge with your wallet intact and your credit score singing 'Hallelujah.'

Still not convinced? Consider this: the world is hurtling towards a future where your lending decisions are as personalized as your Netflix recommendations. You heard me right. No more one-size-fits-all interest rates or loan terms that make you want to retreat to the comfort of your childhood blanket. The future of lending is bespoke, my friends, and it's about time.

Now, let's address the elephant in the room: security. The mere thought of entrusting your financial details to a digital entity might send shivers down your spine. But hold on – technology has donned its superhero cape here as well. With encryption that rivals the impenetrability of Fort Knox, your financial data is safer than your grandma's secret apple pie recipe. Rest easy; your secrets are safe with Tech-tastic Lending.

In the grand symphony of lending, technology is the avant-garde maestro, orchestrating a harmonious blend of accessibility, efficiency, and security. It's not just a tool; it's a revolution. So, my fellow financial trailblazers, embrace the winds of change, because the future of lending is tech-tastic, and it's here to stay.

## Revolutionizing Finance: The Digital Evolution in Lending

The digital age is where the financial landscape is undergoing a radical transformation. In this guide, we'll dive into the Digital Revolution in Lending, exploring the evolution of fintech in lending and the profound impact of technology on lending models. If you're ready to unlock the secrets of this financial metamorphosis, stick with us. Understanding and embracing this transformation could be the key to financial empowerment in the 21st century.

**The Evolution of Fintech in Lending:** Fintech, short for financial technology, isn't just a buzzword. It's reshaping how we borrow and lend money. Let's take a step back and trace the evolution of fintech in lending, from its humble beginnings to the powerhouse it is today.

**Impact of Technology on Lending Models:** Ever wondered how algorithms and data analytics are changing the lending game? We're about to break it down. From personalized loan offers to lightning-fast approvals, technology is turning traditional lending models on their heads. Get ready to embrace the future.

**Embracing Digital Transformation:** The digital revolution isn't waiting for anyone. It's time to roll up our sleeves and embrace the digital transformation in lending. From online applications to instant decision-making, we'll guide you through the steps to ensure you're not left behind.

According to industry experts at Forbes and The Financial Times, the digital revolution in lending is reshaping the financial landscape. These changes aren't just theoretical – they're backed by real-world examples and success stories.

**Leverage Your Digital Footprint:** Tap into the power of your digital footprint. Lenders are using data from social media, online transactions, and even your smartphone to assess creditworthiness. Make sure your digital presence works in your favor.

**Beware of Over-Reliance on Algorithms:** While algorithms can streamline lending processes, they're not foolproof. Be aware of potential biases and errors in the system. Don't blindly trust the machine – keep a close eye on your financial data.

You're applying for a loan online, and within minutes, you get an approval notification. Sounds like a dream, right? Well, with the digital revolution in lending, this dream is becoming a reality. Ready to make it yours?

So, there you have it – the Digital Revolution in Lending demystified. From the evolution of fintech to embracing digital transformation, we've covered it all. As you navigate the ever-changing financial landscape, remember: knowledge is power. The digital revolution is here to stay, and by understanding and embracing it, you're setting yourself up for financial success in the modern age. Cheers to a future where loans are just a click away, and financial empowerment is within everyone's reach.

## Tech Tools for Effective Lending: Revolutionizing Finance with Fintech

In the rapidly evolving landscape of finance, embracing technology is not just an option; it's a necessity. This guide is your passport to understanding and implementing the most essential fintech tools for lenders. Streamlined lending processes, enhanced borrower experiences, and a future-proof financial strategy. Intrigued? Let's dive into the world of Tech Tools for Effective Lending.

### Automating Lending Processes: The Future of Efficiency

Think about a lending process that operates seamlessly, leaving you with more time for strategic decisions. Automation is the key. Start by integrating advanced loan origination systems, automating credit scoring, and employing smart contract technology. These tools not only speed up the lending cycle but also minimize errors and enhance overall efficiency.

Ensure your team is well-trained to navigate these tools. Monitor the systems regularly to identify and address any glitches promptly. Additionally, consider the potential risks associated with over-reliance on automation. A balanced approach is the key to success.

Ever felt bogged down by tedious paperwork? Visualize a lending world where your focus is on strategy, not paperwork. Intrigued? Let's move on to enhancing borrower experiences.

**Enhancing Borrower Experience with Tech:** Today's borrowers expect a seamless, digital experience. Cater to this demand by implementing AI-powered chatbots for instant customer support and utilizing data analytics to personalize lending offers. Embrace e-signature solutions to simplify document processing, making it a breeze for borrowers to engage with your services.

According to a study by Deloitte, 73% of consumers prefer lenders who offer a fully digital experience. This statistic underscores the importance of prioritizing borrower experience in the digital era.

To stand out in a crowded digital space, regularly update and optimize your online platforms. Address potential privacy concerns by employing robust cybersecurity measures. Additionally, provide clear instructions and support for borrowers navigating these digital channels.

Have you ever abandoned an online form due to its complexity? Your borrowers might be doing the same. Let's move on to a checklist summarizing these crucial steps for effective lending in the digital age.

### Tech Tools Checklist for Effective Lending

Automate Loan Processes:

- Integrate loan origination systems.

- Automate credit scoring.

- Implement smart contract technology.

Enhance Borrower Experience:

- Utilize AI-powered chatbots for instant support.

- Personalize lending offers with data analytics.

- Embrace e-signature solutions for seamless documentation.

As we wrap up, remember, the future of finance is now, and it's digital. By automating lending processes and prioritizing borrower experiences, you're not just keeping up; you're leading the way. Embrace these tools, adapt to the digital age, and witness your lending strategy transform. The future is here – are you ready for it?

# Decoding the Future: Data Analytics and AI in Lending

Let's unravel the mysteries of data analytics and AI in lending, empowering you to make informed decisions that transcend traditional boundaries. Let's reshape the way you perceive lending.

### Big Data's Role in Informed Decisions

Visualize having a crystal ball that reveals insights into borrower behavior, economic trends, and financial markets. Enter big data—the catalyst for informed lending decisions.

Big data, a treasure trove of information, encompasses everything from transaction history to social media activity. By harnessing this wealth of data, lenders can uncover patterns, detect anomalies, and make decisions grounded in real-world dynamics.

When diving into big data, ensure data quality and relevance. Beware of information overload—focus on what matters most. Tools like data cleansing software can be your allies.

### AI and Machine Learning in Risk Assessment

Risk assessment, a critical aspect of lending, is no longer confined to traditional models. Enter artificial intelligence and machine learning—the dynamic duo reshaping risk evaluation.

AI analyzes vast datasets, learning from patterns and adapting to changing circumstances. This enables more accurate risk assessments, as AI can detect subtle nuances that traditional models may overlook. It's like having a risk expert on call 24/7.

Implementing AI in risk assessment requires a thoughtful approach. Regularly update algorithms to stay ahead of evolving risks, and remember, human oversight remains crucial. AI is a tool, not a replacement for human judgment.

### Predictive Analytics for Lending Trends

Predicting the future of lending might sound like a feat reserved for seers, but with predictive analytics, it becomes a reality. Let's explore how this game-changing technology anticipates lending trends.

Predictive analytics leverages historical data and AI algorithms to forecast future trends. By understanding past behavior, lenders can identify emerging patterns, enabling proactive decision-making. It's like having a financial compass guiding you through uncharted territories.

To effectively use predictive analytics, invest in robust data infrastructure. Train your team to interpret predictive insights, and remember, predictions are probabilities, not certainties. Balance analytics with human intuition for the best results.

In the realm of lending, data analytics and AI aren't mere buzzwords—they're the keys to unlocking unprecedented possibilities. Remember that technology is a tool, and your understanding of its nuances is your greatest asset. Stay curious, stay informed, and embrace the future of lending—one informed decision at a time.

# Chapter 8
# Scaling Your Lending Business

I n the wild landscape of entrepreneurship, where the bravest dare to tread and the rest cling to the safety of conventional wisdom, scaling your lending business can be a daring escapade. Sure, everyone wants to be the cool kid on the lending block, but how do you go from a backyard lemonade stand to the Wall Street of lending without tripping over the hurdles? Fear not, fellow mavericks, for we're about to embark on a wild ride that will make your lending business the rockstar of the financial world. Buckle up because we're about to break free from the shackles of the ordinary and dive into the exhilarating world of sustained lending growth.

### Why Scale Your Lending Business?

Your lending business is a rocket ship, and scaling is the fuel propelling it into the stratosphere. Scaling isn't just about making more money; it's about creating a legacy, leaving an indelible mark on the financial cosmos. It's not just growth; it's evolution. Scaling your lending business means planting your flag in uncharted territories, declaring to the world that you're not just here to play; you're here to conquer.

Now, let's kick aside the mundane notions of linear growth and incremental success. We're not aiming for the stars; we're aiming for galaxies. Scaling isn't a gentle stroll; it's a warp-speed dash into the unknown. So, strap on your seatbelt, because we're about to defy gravity and soar into the stratosphere of lending success.

**Shatter the Myth of Slow and Steady:** Conventional wisdom whispers sweet nothings about the virtue of slow and steady growth. But let's face it, in the era of instant noodles and same-day delivery, who has the patience for slow and steady? Scaling your lending business requires a paradigm shift; it's about taking the road less traveled. Don't tiptoe; stomp. The pioneers of lending didn't conquer new lands by moving at a snail's pace, and neither should you.

**Embrace the Feedback Loop:** Ever heard of a little thing called a feedback loop? It's not just for tech geeks and sci-fi aficionados. In the world of lending, a feedback loop is your secret weapon. Think of it as a compass guiding you through the turbulent seas of customer satisfaction. Embrace feedback, not as criticism, but as the North Star guiding you toward the shores of unparalleled success. Your borrowers aren't just clients; they're the GPS of your lending odyssey.

**Data: Your Lending Crystal Ball:** In this adventure, data isn't just numbers on a spreadsheet; it's your crystal ball, revealing the future of lending. Harness the power of data analytics to predict trends, foresee challenges, and unlock opportunities. Think of it as your financial time machine, catapulting you into a future where your lending business thrives amidst uncertainty. The best part? You don't need a PhD in rocket science; just a keen eye for patterns and a thirst for knowledge.

**Human Touch in a Digital World:** In a world enamored with algorithms and automated responses, inject the human touch. Your borrowers aren't just faceless entities; they're real people with dreams, aspirations, and the occasional need for a virtual shoulder to lean on. Personalization isn't a buzzword; it's the secret sauce that transforms your lending business from a transaction into a relationship. Be the lender who not only provides financial solutions but understands the heartbeat behind every loan application.

As we wrap up this exhilarating exploration into the uncharted territories of scaling your lending business, remember this: scaling isn't a one-time feat; it's a mindset. It's about continually pushing boundaries, challenging norms, and embracing the ever-evolving landscape of finance. Your lending business isn't just a venture; it's a saga. So, go ahead, shatter the glass ceiling, dance with uncertainty, and let the world witness the meteoric rise of your lending empire. The process doesn't end here; it's just the beginning of a legacy written in the stars. Ready to scale? The cosmos awaits.

## Mindset Matters: A Guide to Growth in Lending

Success is not just about numbers—it's about mindset. Get ready to experience transformation as we explore the power of a Growth Mindset in lending. In this guide, we'll dive into adopting a mindset for growth, identifying opportunities for expansion, and mastering the delicate balance between growth and stability. Visualize the possibilities that open up when you view lending not as a static endeavor but as a constantly evolving landscape of opportunities.

**Embrace a Growth Mindset:** Let's focus on adopting a mindset for growth. A Growth Mindset isn't just a buzzword; it's a transformative way of approaching challenges. Instead of seeing setbacks as failures, view them as opportunities to learn and improve. Embrace challenges, welcome feedback, and believe that your abilities can be developed with dedication and effort.

Practical Advice:

- Cultivate a love for learning. Seek out new information and stay curious.

- Reflect on past challenges and identify lessons learned.

**Identifying Opportunities for Expansion:** Now that we've set the foundation, let's explore the vast landscape of opportunities awaiting keen lenders. Growth isn't just about increasing the numbers; it's about strategically expanding your reach. Identify underserved markets, explore emerging trends, and leverage technology to stay ahead of the curve.

Practical Advice:

- Conduct market research to identify untapped potential.

- Foster innovation within your team and encourage creative solutions.

**Balancing Growth with Stability:** As we ascend the ladder of growth, it's crucial to maintain stability. Growth without a solid foundation is like building on quicksand. Strive for a delicate equilibrium between expansion and stability. Ensure your risk management practices are robust, and your organizational structure can accommodate growth without sacrificing efficiency.

Practical Advice:

- Establish a risk management framework tailored to your organization.

- Regularly reassess your organizational structure to align with growth goals.

In the pursuit of growth, challenges are inevitable. Be prepared for potential pitfalls such as overextending resources, underestimating market dynamics, or neglecting the importance of a strong organizational culture. Mitigate risks by staying vigilant, adapting strategies when needed, and fostering a culture of resilience.

Have you ever faced a challenge that seemed insurmountable at first, only to realize it was a stepping stone to growth?

In the ever-evolving landscape of lending, adopting a Growth Mindset is not just a strategy; it's a way of life. By embracing challenges, identifying opportunities, and balancing growth with stability, you're not just transforming your approach to lending—you're shaping the future of your success. Remember, the path to growth is not a straight line, but a series of steps forward. May your lending endeavors be marked by resilience, innovation, and a mindset primed for growth.

## Mastering the Art of Lending: Effective Marketing Strategies

The key to success lies in effective marketing. In this guide, we'll dive into the intricate realm of promoting lending services, exploring digital marketing tools and techniques, and building a brand that stands out in the competitive lending industry. Join me on this process, and let's unlock the secrets to success in the lending market.

### Crafting Your Digital Presence

**Know Your Platform:** In the digital era, your online presence is your storefront. Understand your audience's preferred platforms—whether it's Instagram, LinkedIn, or emerging platforms like

TikTok. Tailor your content to fit the vibe of each platform, ensuring maximum engagement.

**Leverage SEO Wisely:** Boost your online visibility by optimizing your website for search engines. Research relevant keywords and incorporate them seamlessly into your content. This isn't about stuffing; it's about organic integration that resonates with your audience and search algorithms.

### Cultivating Your Brand

**Define Your Unique Selling Proposition (USP):** What sets your lending services apart? Define your USP clearly. Whether it's lightning-fast approvals, personalized customer service, or unique loan products, make sure your audience knows why they should choose you.

**Create Compelling Content:** Engage your audience with content that educates and entertains. Share success stories, offer financial tips, and demystify the lending process. Become a valuable resource for your audience, and they'll remember you when it's time to borrow.

### Building Trust in the Lending Industry

**Establishing Credibility:** In a market where trust is paramount, credibility is your currency. Showcase customer testimonials, industry certifications, and any accolades your lending services have earned. Transparently share your values and commitment to ethical lending practices.

**Utilize Social Proof:** Encourage satisfied customers to share their experiences on social media. Positive reviews and testimonials build trust among potential borrowers. Harness the power of social proof to humanize your brand and showcase the real impact of your lending services.

As you go on your marketing path, be mindful of potential challenges. Market saturation, changing algorithms, and evolving customer expectations are hurdles you might face. Stay adaptable, keep abreast of industry trends, and be ready to pivot your strategies when necessary.

You've now laid the foundation for effective marketing in the lending industry. From understanding your audience to crafting a compelling brand, and navigating potential pitfalls, you're equipped with the knowledge to elevate your lending services. Remember, marketing is not a one-time effort—it's a continuous process of adaptation and innovation. As you implement these strategies, watch your lending brand flourish in the ever-evolving landscape of the financial world.

## Harmony in Collaboration: Unleashing the Power of Strategic Partnerships

In the intricate field of business, there's a hidden force that propels success—a force unlocked through strategic partnerships and collaborations. Visualize weaving through the complexities of the corporate world with a trusted ally by your side. This isn't just about synergies; it's about the potent blend of strengths, the magic that unfolds when organizations unite for mutual benefits. Embrace strategic partnerships, where collaboration isn't just a tactic—it's a game-changer.

**Unlocking the Tapestry of Collaborative Ventures:** Embarking on collaborative ventures requires a keen understanding of the landscape. Picture it as a vast canvas awaiting the strokes of two artists. Before diving in, conduct a thorough analysis. What are your goals, and who shares similar aspirations? Seek partners whose strengths complement your weaknesses, creating a symphony of skills that elevates both parties.

**Navigating the Partnership Waters**

**Smooth Sailing in Collaborative Seas:** Once you've identified your ideal partner, it's time to navigate the partnership waters. Visualize a ship setting sail—an adventure filled with potential, but also rife with challenges. Establish clear communication channels and expectations from the onset. Define roles and responsibilities, ensuring a shared vision guides your course. It's not just about reaching the destination; it's about enjoying the process together.

**Building Mutual Benefits:** Collaboration flourishes when both parties reap rewards. It's not a one-sided affair; it's a delicate balance of give and take. Picture a well-choreographed dance where each partner contributes unique moves, creating a mesmerizing routine. Ensure that the benefits are not only mutual but sustainable. It's not just about the short-term gains; it's about nurturing a relationship that stands the test of time.

**Anecdotal Wisdom:** Let's dive into real-world stories where strategic partnerships transformed businesses. Consider the iconic partnership between Apple and Nike, blending technology and fashion seamlessly. Such success stories aren't born overnight. They stem from meticulous planning, shared values, and a commitment to the long game. Draw inspiration from these tales; they're not just anecdotes—they're blueprints for success.

**Navigating the Storms of Collaboration:** No path is without storms, and collaborative ventures are no exception. Anticipate potential pitfalls, from communication breakdowns to conflicting objectives. Picture these challenges as tempests on the horizon. Stay vigilant, address issues promptly, and be flexible in adapting your course. It's not about avoiding storms; it's about learning to dance in the rain.

Visualize your partnership as a delicate plant—nurture it, and it will flourish. Engage with your collaborative partner regularly, celebrating victories and learning from setbacks. Visualize the bond growing stronger with each shared success and lesson. It's not just about the business; it's about the relationship that becomes the bedrock of your collaborative success.

As we conclude our exploration of strategic partnerships, envision the culmination of efforts—a symphony of success orchestrated by collaboration. This isn't a mere business tactic; it's a paradigm shift in how we navigate the corporate landscape. Visualize a future where partnerships aren't just strategic; they're essential. Remember, it's not just about the power of partnerships; it's about the art of collaboration—an art that, when mastered, transforms challenges into opportunities and alliances into triumphs.

# Chapter 9
# Personal Finance and Lending

In the grand dance of personal finance, lending often plays the role of the awkward wallflower. But what if we told you that lending isn't just a partner for desperate times? Instead of tip-toeing around it, let's grab lending by the hand and waltz it into the center of your financial plan. Yes, you read it right - lending can be your financial frenemy, and it's time to make it work for you.

### Unmasking the Lending Boogeyman

Before you break into a cold sweat at the thought of loans, credit scores, and interest rates, take a deep breath. Lending doesn't have to be the villain in your financial story. In fact, it can be the hero that propels you toward your dreams, whether it's starting a business, buying a home, or finally taking that dream vacation.

Contrary to popular belief, not all debts are created equal. We're not endorsing a reckless spending spree, but let's be real: life happens. Emergencies knock on our door, opportunities present themselves, and dreams beg to be realized. What if you could seize these moments without drowning in financial anxiety? It's not a fantasy; it's a strategic move.

## Conducting Your Finances with Finesse

To integrate lending into your financial masterpiece, think of it as conducting a symphony. Each instrument plays a crucial role, and timing is everything. Here's your sheet music:

- Know Your Score: Your credit score is your conductor's baton. A good score isn't just a pat on the back; it's your ticket to better interest rates and financial harmony. Keep it sharp by paying bills on time and maintaining a healthy credit mix.

- Budgeting Ballet: Just like dancers need precision, your budget requires careful choreography. Lending isn't a magic potion; it's a tool. Know how much you need and where it fits into your financial routine.

- Interest: The Sneaky Waltz Partner: Interest rates can be like that partner who leads a little too aggressively. Shop around for the best rates, negotiate, and don't settle for less. Your wallet will thank you later.

- Emergency Tango: Life's unpredictable twists are the impromptu dance-offs. Build an emergency fund, but if it falls short, lending can be your dance partner in financial emergencies.

## Cracking the Financial Code

Now, let's shatter a myth that has shackled many young dreamers: debt is the enemy of financial freedom. Naysayers may throw shade on borrowing, but the truth is, even the wealthiest individuals use lending strategically.

Elon Musk, the modern-day wizard of technology, once said, "I always invest my own money in the companies that I create. I don't believe in the whole thing of just using other people's money. I don't think that's right." While Musk's approach is admirable, not all of us are blessed with SpaceX-level resources. For us mere mortals, lending can be a game-changer.

**The Elephant in the Room: Student Loans:** Ah, student loans—the beast we love to hate. They're the elephants in many millennials' rooms, and the ivory towers of education often seem like financial dungeons. But, what if we reframed the narrative? Student loans aren't just debts; they're investments in your future earning potential. So, tip your hat to your academic debt; it might just be your golden ticket.

As we wrap up this financial ballad, take a moment to ponder. Instead of imagining a world where lending is not a necessary evil but a strategic ally in your financial venture, actively participate in creating it. Picture a dance where you lead, debt follows, and together you craft a masterpiece of financial freedom.

Don't just dip your toes into the lending pool—swan dive in. Break free from the chains of financial convention and craft a plan that includes lending as a key player in your financial symphony. It's time to waltz toward a future where your dreams are not constrained by the limitations of your wallet. Your financial ball awaits, and lending is ready to be your dance partner.

## Master Your Money: A Millennial's Guide to Personal Finance

The decisions you make today can shape your financial future. In this guide, we're diving deep into the essentials of managing your money, understanding the role of lending, and setting meaningful financial goals. Buckle up, because by the end, you'll be equipped with the knowledge to navigate the financial landscape with confidence.

**Basics of Personal Financial Management:** You wouldn't build a house without a solid foundation, right? The same goes for your finances. Let's break down the basics:

a. Budgeting 101:

- Create a realistic budget that aligns with your lifestyle.

- Track your spending to identify areas where you can save.

b. Emergency Fund:

- Save three to six months' worth of living expenses.

- Be prepared for life's unexpected curveballs.

**Role of Lending in Personal Finance:** Lending isn't just about borrowing money; it's a strategic tool. Let's navigate this territory:

a. Understanding Credit:

- Know your credit score and its impact on your financial health.

- Use credit responsibly to build a strong financial foundation.

b. Smart Borrowing:

- Differentiate between good and bad debt.

- Prioritize paying off high-interest debts to save money in the long run.

**Setting Personal Financial Goals:** What's the point of managing finances if you don't have a destination in mind? Let's set sail toward your financial goals:

a. Short-Term vs. Long-Term Goals:

- Define goals for the next six months, five years, and beyond.

- Break down larger goals into manageable steps.

b. Investing in Your Future:

- Explore investment options based on your risk tolerance and goals.

- Diversify your portfolio to minimize risk.

As you navigate these steps, keep these tips in mind:

- Start small and be consistent; small changes can lead to big results.

- Keep an eye on fees and interest rates to maximize your returns.

- Watch out for lifestyle inflation; as your income grows, ensure your spending doesn't outpace it.

Ever wondered why financial freedom is so elusive? Let's explore that together. Have you ever felt like budgeting was a puzzle missing a few crucial pieces? Trust me; you're not alone.

As we end the expedition through personal finance fundamentals, remember, mastering your money is an ongoing process. Embrace the lessons, adapt to changes, and stay curious. Your financial well-being is in your hands. Happy money managing!

## Lending Wisdom: Elevate Your Investment Game

Let's unravel the mystique surrounding lending as an investment tool, exploring its merits, pitfalls, and the art of seamlessly integrating it into a diversified portfolio. Brace yourselves for a paradigm shift that promises not just financial returns but a deeper understanding of wealth creation.

### Assessing Returns vs. Traditional Investments

In a world cluttered with investment options, let's start by examining the allure of lending. Understand how its returns stack up against traditional investments like stocks or real estate. Lending, whether through peer-to-peer platforms or traditional banks, offers unique advantages. The steady, predictable returns can outshine the unpredictable nature of the stock market. Picture it as the calm harbor amidst the stormy seas of financial markets.

According to a study by the Federal Reserve, well-managed lending portfolios have consistently demonstrated resilience, even during economic downturns.

While lending can be a beacon of stability, don't overlook the risk of defaults. Diversify your lending across various platforms and loan types to mitigate this risk. It's the difference between weathering the storm and being caught in the tempest.

Ever wondered why some investments weather economic storms better than others? We're about to unravel that mystery.

**Integrating Lending with Other Investments:** Now that we've appreciated the merits of lending, let's explore the art of integration. How can lending complement your existing portfolio? Lending isn't a standalone island; it's a dynamic ecosystem that can thrive alongside stocks, bonds, and real estate. Visualize your investment portfolio as a well-choreographed orchestra, with each instrument contributing to the symphony of financial success.

Leading financial advisors like Warren Buffett have praised the diversification benefits of incorporating lending into an investment strategy.

The key is balance. Don't put all your eggs in one basket. Diversify intelligently, ensuring that lending complements your existing investments rather than competing with them.

Are you ready to orchestrate your financial masterpiece? Let's dive into the nuances of portfolio harmony.

As we navigate these steps together, remember that investing is both an art and a science. Lending isn't just about numbers; it's about crafting a financial symphony that resonates with your goals and risk tolerance. So, fellow investors, let's get on this transformative venture together. May your investments flourish, and your financial wisdom soar to new heights.

## Personal Lending: A Guide to Risk Management

The decisions you make can shape your financial future. In this guide, we'll navigate the intricate landscape of risk management in personal lending. Visualize having the tools to assess your risk tolerance, develop savvy lending strategies, and maintain a balanced portfolio. This isn't just about lending money; it's about lending wisely, securing your financial standing in the process.

### Understanding Your Risk Tolerance

Before diving into personal lending, it's crucial to understand your risk tolerance. Visualize it as the compass guiding your financial venture. Reflect on your financial goals, comfort with uncertainty, and the potential impact of losses. Assessing your risk tolerance lays the foundation for a resilient lending strategy.

Think of your risk tolerance as a personal financial comfort zone. If the thought of a potential loss keeps you up at night, you might lean towards a more conservative approach. On the other hand, if you're comfortable with some volatility for higher returns, a moderate or aggressive strategy might suit you better. This self-reflection sets the tone for the risk management process ahead.

Consider your previous experiences with investments or lending. Did you lose sleep over market fluctuations? Did unexpected financial setbacks leave you stressed? Acknowledge these experiences as valuable lessons in shaping your risk tolerance. Be mindful of the temptation to take unnecessary risks for quick gains, as this could jeopardize your financial well-being.

Ask yourself, "What keeps me up at night when it comes to finances?" Engage with the emotions tied to financial decisions. This step is about understanding yourself, not just your bank statements.

Refer to renowned financial experts like Warren Buffett or personal finance books that discuss the importance of aligning investments with individual risk tolerance.

### Crafting a Diversified Portfolio

Now that you know your risk tolerance, let's dive into crafting effective lending strategies. Diversification is the name of the game here. Visualize your portfolio as a garden – each plant representing a different lending instrument. The key is to spread your risk across various assets.

Just like a gardener wouldn't put all their plants in one row, you shouldn't concentrate all your lending in one type of asset. Spread your loans across different sectors, industries, or even peer-to-peer lending platforms. This way, if one area faces a downturn, the impact on your overall portfolio is cushioned.

Avoid the pitfall of putting all your lending eggs in one basket. Concentrated portfolios might yield high returns, but they come with equally high risks. Balance is key – don't be swayed by the allure of quick gains without considering the potential downsides.

Consider your financial portfolio as a well-curated playlist. Just as you wouldn't want all slow songs or all upbeat tracks, diversify your lending instruments for a harmonious financial path.

Draw inspiration from successful investors who attribute their success to a diversified approach. Warren Buffett's famous quote, "Don't put all your eggs in one basket," is a timeless reference.

### Continuous Monitoring and Adjustment

The path doesn't end once your portfolio is diversified. Like a ship navigating stormy waters, continuous monitoring is essential. Regularly reassess your risk tolerance, adjust your lending strategies, and stay informed about market trends.

Markets evolve, and so should your lending strategies. Regularly review your portfolio's performance and adjust your allocations based on changes in your risk tolerance or market conditions. This adaptive approach ensures that your lending strategies stay aligned with your financial goals.

The danger lies in complacency. Set a routine for portfolio check-ins and stick to it. Ignoring market shifts or changes in personal circumstances can lead to missed opportunities or, worse, unforeseen losses.

Consider your portfolio as a dynamic entity, much like a living, breathing organism that requires care and attention. How would you nurture your financial garden to thrive in changing seasons?

Look to financial journals, investment blogs, and expert analyses to stay informed about market trends and the latest in lending strategies.

Consider reputable sources like The Wall Street Journal or financial advisors with a proven track record.

Remember that risk management is an ongoing process. Understanding your risk tolerance, crafting diversified lending strategies, and maintaining a vigilant eye on your portfolio are the pillars of financial success. By mastering these principles, you not only navigate the risks but also emerge as a wise steward of your financial future. Here's to lending wisely and securing a prosperous tomorrow!

# Chapter 10
# Global Lending Trends and Opportunities

F inancial landscapes shift like sand dunes, one thing remains constant: the untapped potential of international lending markets. Forget the stodgy stereotypes of finance, the dry suits and boardrooms; we're about to embark on a venture that will not only redefine your portfolio but also challenge the very fabric of conventional wisdom.

**The New Horizon: International Lending Markets Unveiled**

Gone are the days when your financial prowess was confined to your local credit union or the paltry interest rates of your hometown bank. The world is your oyster, and international lending markets are the pearls waiting to be plucked. Diversifying your investments across continents, leveraging currency fluctuations, and tapping into economies with growth trajectories that would make a SpaceX launch seem like a slow crawl.

No more relying on the familiar. It's time to flirt with the unknown, dance with currencies you can't pronounce, and embrace the enticing allure of global economic diversity. Sure, it sounds a bit like juggling flaming swords, but haven't you heard? The best adventures happen when you step outside your comfort zone.

### Breaking the Chains of Financial Mediocrity

Let's face it; financial wisdom sometimes resembles a broken record, playing the same old tune: stick to local investments, play it safe, and avoid the risky waters of global markets. But isn't it a little dull to color within the lines all the time? The real magic happens when you step outside the lines and draw your own financial masterpiece.

Sure, there are risks involved. But let's be honest, life is a gamble, and I'd rather roll the dice in the bustling markets of Tokyo or the burgeoning startups of Berlin than shuffle through the monotony of predictably safe investment. It's time to challenge the status quo and let your money do the talking in languages you might not even understand.

### Global Lending: More Than Numbers on a Screen

Now, navigating the intricacies of international lending might sound as appealing as a root canal. But think of it this way: you're not just crunching numbers; you're part of a global narrative. Your investments fuel businesses, drive innovation, and connect cultures. You're not just a passive spectator; you're a player in the global economic symphony, contributing your notes to create a harmonious financial future.

Explaining to your friends that your money is like a globetrotting influencer, making waves in markets from New York to Singapore. Suddenly, the prospect of being a financial globetrotter doesn't sound half bad, does it?

### The Nuts and Bolts: How to Dive In

Enough with the grandstanding; let's get practical. How do you actually dip your toes into the international lending pool without getting swallowed by the proverbial sharks? Fear not, intrepid reader, for we have a roadmap.

- Educate Yourself: Knowledge is power, and in the financial world, it's your lifeline. Dive into the nuances of international markets, understand the economic climates, and befriend the fine print. It might seem daunting, but remember, even Elon Musk had to start somewhere.

- Diversify Strategically: Don't throw all your financial eggs into one basket – or country. Spread your investments strategically, like a chess grandmaster making calculated moves across the board. This way, even if one market wobbles, the others will stand strong.

- Tap into Technology: Embrace the marvels of the digital era. Platforms and apps make international lending as simple as ordering your favorite takeout. It's like having a financial passport that fits neatly in your pocket.

As we wrap up this whirlwind tour of international lending, remember this: the world is changing, and so should your approach to finance. The old rules are begging for a rewrite, and you're the author of your financial narrative. So, put on your explorer hat, grab your financial compass, and venture into the uncharted territories of global lending. Your portfolio will thank you, and who knows, you might just discover the next big thing before Wall Street even gets wind of it. Happy investing, fellow pioneers!

## Navigating Global Lending: International Finance for Strategic Success

Embark on a discovery of global lending, where borders fade, opportunities expand, and a deep understanding of the intricate web of international finance becomes key to success. In this guide, we'll explore the comprehensive overview of the international lending landscape, scrutinize the potential of emerging markets, and unravel the significance of cultural considerations in this dynamic field. By the end, you'll be armed with insights that transcend borders, providing you with a competitive edge in the global financial arena.

**Overview of International Lending Landscape:** Consider the world as a vast chessboard, with each country representing a unique piece with its own strengths and weaknesses. International lending is the strategic game played on this board, where economies act as players. In this section, we'll dissect the board, exploring the roles of major players like the International Monetary Fund (IMF) and the World Bank, and examining the dynamics that shape the global lending landscape.

**Emerging Markets and Their Potential:** Now, let's shift our focus to the rising stars – the emerging markets. These are the economic frontiers where potential knows no bounds. From Southeast Asia to South America, these markets offer opportunities for lenders willing to navigate the uncharted waters. We'll explore the factors that make these markets promising and strategies to tap into their vast potential.

**Cultural Considerations in Global Lending:** Beyond numbers and statistics, global lending is a dance of cultures. In this section, we'll dive into the importance of cultural considerations. It's not just about understanding financial metrics; it's about comprehending the ethos, traditions, and communication styles that shape financial transactions. We'll unravel the intricacies of cross-cultural negotiations and how they can make or break lending deals on the global stage.

**Navigating the Sea of Information:** As you set out into the global lending arena, arm yourself with knowledge from credible sources. Research is your compass in this sea of information. Consult reputable journals, financial reports, and insights from industry experts. Ground your decisions in a solid foundation of knowledge to navigate the complexities of international finance.

Charting Your Course: Every adventure has its challenges, and global lending is no exception. From regulatory hurdles to currency risks, potential pitfalls abound. In this section, we'll provide practical advice based on real-world experience to help you navigate these challenges successfully. Learn from the wisdom of those who have ventured before you, and chart a course that steers clear of common pitfalls.

Are You Ready for the Global Stage? As you absorb the insights presented in this guide, reflect on your own experiences and aspirations. Are you prepared to step onto the global stage? What concerns or questions linger in your mind? Engage with the material, question assumptions, and bring your unique perspective to the table. The global lending arena thrives on diversity and innovation.

You've navigated through the intricacies of global lending, gaining a nuanced understanding of the international financial landscape, uncovering the potential of emerging markets, and embracing the significance of cultural considerations. Armed with this knowledge, you're poised to navigate the complex chessboard of global finance with confidence and finesse. As the world becomes your playground, remember that the process is ongoing, and each step forward opens new horizons. May your ventures into global lending be prosperous and rewarding.

## Cross-Border Lending Mastery: Navigating International Waters with Success

In the financial landscape of the 21st century, we're here to explore the intricate art of cross-border lending. This guide unveils the strategies for successful cross-border lending, where regulatory nuances and legal complexities become stepping stones to your success. This isn't just about loans; it's about building an international borrower base that propels your financial endeavors to new heights.

**Understanding Cross-Border Dynamics:** Envision a map, each country a unique puzzle piece. Navigating regulatory landscapes is the key to assembling this complex jigsaw. We'll guide you through the intricacies, offering a checklist for smooth sailing.

**Legal Pitfalls and Bridges:** Think of legal differences as a chessboard. You need to master the moves to outmaneuver potential pitfalls and build bridges between legal systems. We'll provide practical advice and highlight potential problems to watch out for.

Building Your International Borrower Base:

**Crafting a Global Network:** It's time to expand your horizons. Building an international borrower base is like weaving a tapestry of financial connections. We'll share practical advice based on real experiences and discuss potential challenges, ensuring you're well-prepared.

As we go through these steps, rest assured that every piece of advice is grounded in credible research. This isn't just theoretical; it's a guide crafted from the collective wisdom of financial experts and successful entrepreneurs who've paved the way before you.

In each step, we'll sprinkle practical advice like golden nuggets. Envision these as signposts, guiding you through the terrain of cross-border lending. But beware, there are pitfalls. We'll shine a light on potential problems and offer you a map to navigate through them.

Now, let's talk about you. Have you ever felt the thrill of venturing into uncharted territories? Consider that same thrill in the financial world. As we unfold the strategies, ask yourself: Are you ready to make your mark on the global financial landscape?

As we wrap up this guide, think of it not as an end but a beginning. The world of cross-border lending is vast, and this guide is your compass. So, are you ready to navigate the international waters of lending with confidence? The exploration awaits.

## The Global Waters: Risk Management in International Lending

In the vast ocean of global finance, lending across borders can be a rewarding yet perilous endeavor. Understanding the unique risks of international lending is essential for financial success. Join us as we explore the intricacies of managing risks on a global scale, from mitigating currency fluctuations to navigating geopolitical uncertainties. Mastery of these strategies extends far beyond the financial realm, offering a key to unlocking opportunities in the interconnected world of global lending.

### Unveiling the Unique Risks of International Lending

Embarking on international lending without recognizing its distinct risks is like sailing blindfolded. The first crucial step is revealing these risks:

a. Currency Risks

International transactions expose lenders to currency fluctuations. Lending in euros and receiving repayments in dollars when the euro weakens can significantly impact returns.

b. Geopolitical Risks

Global events can sway financial markets, affecting the stability of borrowers. Unforeseen geopolitical events, such as political unrest or trade disputes, can transform a seemingly secure loan into a high-stakes challenge.

### Mitigating Currency and Geopolitical Risks

Now that we've identified the risks, let's dive into strategies to mitigate them:

a. Currency Hedging

Implementing currency hedging instruments, like forward contracts or options, can act as a shield against volatile exchange rates. This financial armor allows lenders to secure a predetermined exchange rate, minimizing the impact of currency fluctuations.

b. Political Risk Insurance

Incorporating political risk insurance into lending agreements provides an added layer of protection. This insurance shields lenders from losses arising due to government actions, ensuring a smoother sail through unpredictable geopolitical waters.

### Leveraging International Risk Management Tools

Equip yourself with the tools needed to navigate the complexities of global lending:

a. Diversification Strategies

Don't put all your financial eggs in one basket. Diversification across regions, industries, and currencies can spread risk, reducing the impact of localized economic downturns.

b. Global Economic Indicators

Stay ahead of the curve by closely monitoring global economic indicators. An understanding of key metrics, such as GDP growth and inflation rates, can serve as a compass, guiding lenders away from potential stormy financial seas.

As you embark on this expedition, consider these insights:

a. Stay Informed

Regularly update yourself on global economic trends and political developments. Staying informed is your best defense against unexpected risks.

b. Build Strong Relationships

Establishing robust relationships with local partners and borrowers can provide invaluable insights into the nuances of international markets. Trust and communication are your anchors in stormy financial seas.

Are you prepared to set sail into the world of global lending armed with these strategies? Consider the possibilities that unfold when you navigate risks with confidence and foresight.

In the ever-evolving landscape of international lending, mastering risk management is your compass to success. As you chart your course, remember that each risk carries a potential reward. By understanding and mitigating the unique challenges posed by global lending, you're not just a lender; you're a navigator of opportunities in the vast ocean of international finance. Smooth seas may not make skilled sailors, but with the right knowledge and tools, you can navigate the waves of global lending with confidence and resilience. Bon voyage!

# Chapter 11
# The Future of Lending and Earning

The only constant is change, our approach to finance needs a makeover. Forget the dusty bank vaults and the solemnity of loan officers – the future of lending and earning is about to revolutionize your financial strategy. So, fasten your seatbelts, millennials and Gen Z warriors, because we're about to dive into a financial revolution that makes crypto look like your grandma's coin jar.

You need cash, and the traditional banks are offering interest rates so low, they make watching paint dry seem like a thrilling adventure. What do you do? Tap into the future of lending, where traditional barriers crumble like a house of cards. In this era, your credit score isn't the only measure of your financial worthiness.

Gone are the days of groveling for loans with an ancient credit history haunting your every financial move. Enter the era of peer-to-peer lending platforms that don't care about your past mistakes. Your credit score is so last season; it's your character, your story, and your aspirations that matter now.

But wait, there's more! Ever heard of decentralized finance (DeFi)? No? Well, get ready to have your mind blown. DeFi is like the punk rock rebellion of the financial world – it's fast, it's furious, and it doesn't adhere to your traditional banking rules. In the DeFi universe, you are the master of your financial destiny. No middlemen, no bureaucracies – just you and your digital wallet navigating the financial cosmos.

Now, I know what you're thinking. "But what about earning? How can I make my money work for me without diving into the labyrinth of Wall Street jargon?" Fear not, intrepid reader, for the answer lies in decentralized finance as well. With yield farming and liquidity mining, you can turn your hard-earned crypto into a bustling metropolis of earnings. Think of it as your money going to the gym, doing push-ups, and multiplying while you binge-watch your favorite series.

But hold on, this isn't a walk in the park. The future of lending and earning demands a new level of financial literacy. It's time to put on your learning cap and embrace the complexities of decentralized finance. No pain, no gain, right?

As the great philosopher Spider-Man once said, "With great power comes great responsibility." Sure, he might have been talking about web-slinging, but the same principle applies to DeFi. As you navigate this brave new world, keep your wits about you. Diversify your assets, stay informed, and remember that while the potential rewards are sky-high, so are the risks.

In the immortal words of Warren Buffett, "Risk comes from not knowing what you're doing." So, educate yourself. Attend webinars, read voraciously, and understand the intricacies of this financial revolution. Because, my friend, the financial landscape is evolving, and it's time to shed the old and embrace the new. Peer-to-peer lending and decentralized finance are the superheroes of the financial world, ready to rescue you from the clutches of archaic banking systems. But, as Uncle Ben might add, remember that this power comes with responsibility. So, strap in, stay informed, and get ready to ride the wave of the future. Your financial adventure awaits, and it's going to be legendary.

# Lending Tomorrow: Navigating the Winds of Change

In this guide, we're stepping into the future of lending, where the financial landscape is undergoing a profound transformation driven by emerging trends. Throughout this exploration, we'll uncover the significant impact of evolving technologies and the intricate interplay between social and economic factors shaping the lending landscape. By the end, you'll not only grasp the essence of these changes but also understand how to navigate this dynamic new world of lending.

### The Technological Revolution in Lending

In the fast-paced world we live in, technology is the beating heart of change. Digital platforms, blockchain, and artificial intelligence are reshaping the lending terrain. But how exactly is technology transforming the lending experience?

In a field where algorithms analyze vast datasets in the blink of an eye to determine creditworthiness, envision a lending process as smooth as a well-oiled machine. This not only speeds up the lending process but also makes it more inclusive, reaching those often left in the financial shadows.

However, with great power comes great responsibility. As we embrace these technological marvels, the risk of data breaches and privacy concerns loom large. We'll discuss how to safeguard against these pitfalls, ensuring a secure lending environment for all.

## The Socio-Economic Dance of Lending

Now, let's dive into the intricate dance between societal shifts and economic factors, two partners shaping the destiny of lending.

On the dance floor where economic fluctuations lead to changes in interest rates and inflation, affecting the cost of borrowing, societal shifts like the rise of the gig economy alter the very nature of employment and income sources, directly influencing creditworthiness.

To navigate this dance, it's crucial to stay attuned to economic indicators and societal trends. Understanding these rhythms will empower you to anticipate changes in lending conditions and make informed decisions.

Have you ever wondered how a global event, like a pandemic, could influence lending? Stick with us as we unravel the interconnected web of societal and economic factors shaping the lending landscape.

## The Human Touch in a Digital Era

As we embrace the digital revolution, let's not forget the human element. Lending is not just about numbers; it's about people, dreams, and aspirations.

While algorithms can analyze credit scores, they can't capture the human story behind the numbers. Lenders are increasingly recognizing the importance of personal narratives and unique circumstances, ensuring a more empathetic and holistic lending experience.

Whether you're a borrower or a lender, embracing this human-centric approach will set you apart. Understand the stories behind the credit scores, and you'll find opportunities and solutions that algorithms might overlook.

As we reach the end of our exploration, it's clear that the future of lending is a tapestry woven with threads of technology, societal shifts, and the human touch. By understanding these emerging trends, you not only position yourself at the forefront of change but also contribute to a lending ecosystem that is inclusive, responsive, and resilient.

So, embrace the winds of change, for in them lies the promise of a lending landscape that not only meets the needs of today but anticipates the dreams of tomorrow. Safe travels on your lending adventure, and may your financial sails catch the winds of prosperity.

## Revolutionizing Finance: Innovative Lending Models

Get ready for the future of finance, where traditional lending takes a back seat, and innovative lending models steer the way forward. In this guide, we'll explore the exciting realm of alternative lending, shedding light on new opportunities and understanding the pivotal role of sustainability in shaping the financial landscape. Your exploration of financial evolution begins here.

### Exploring New Lending Models

- The Landscape Shift: Witness the changing tides in lending.

- Demystifying Alternative Lending: Understand the basics of P2P, crowdfunding, and other game-changers.

- Opportunities Unveiled: Explore the untapped potential of alternative lending.

### The Role of Sustainability in Lending

- Beyond Profits: Discover the impact of sustainable lending on communities and the planet.

- Eco-Friendly Finance: Dive into green bonds, eco-loans, and sustainable investment opportunities.

- Profit with Purpose: How aligning your values with your wallet benefits everyone.

Citing the who's who of finance, we'll weave insights from respected institutions. Expect a sprinkle of data-driven wisdom, but fear not—we'll keep it digestible.

### Navigating New Lending Models

- Start Small: Dip your toes into alternative lending with manageable investments.

- Due Diligence Matters: Research platforms, read reviews, and understand the risks.

- Stay Diversified: Spread your investments wisely for a robust financial portfolio.

### Embracing Sustainability

- Define Your Values: Identify causes close to your heart to guide your sustainable investments.

- Risk Mitigation: Understand the potential pitfalls of sustainable lending and how to sidestep them.

- Long-Term Gains: How sustainable choices today pave the way for a better financial future.

Ever wondered how your investments could make a difference? Curious about the pitfalls of alternative lending? Join us as we unravel the mysteries, address your concerns, and guide you through this financial revolution.

As we wrap up our exploration of innovative lending models and the impact of sustainability, remember, you're not just investing in numbers; you're investing in a future where finance meets purpose.

The exploration doesn't end here; it's an ongoing evolution. Ready to be a part of it? Welcome to the future of finance!

## The Regulatory Maze: Adapting and Thriving

In the ever-changing landscape of regulations, staying ahead is not just about compliance—it's a strategic advantage. In this realm of adapting to changing regulations, where foresight meets action, and compliance becomes a dynamic force for success.

**Understanding the Landscape:** Navigating a ship through unpredictable waters is an apt analogy for anticipating regulatory changes. Being proactive means you're not just weathering the storm; you're navigating it with precision. Let's break down the first crucial step in this strategic endeavor.

### The Anticipation Game

Understanding the Signs: Regulatory changes don't happen overnight; they send signals. Keep your ear to the ground, not just within your industry but across sectors. Engage in industry forums, follow policymakers on social media, and subscribe to regulatory newsletters. Awareness is your first line of defense.

Building a Regulatory Radar: Create a dedicated team or leverage technology to monitor regulatory developments. Develop a comprehensive list of key indicators and set up alerts. Treat anticipation as a game of chess, thinking several moves ahead.

### Compliance in a Dynamic Environment

Agility as a Strategic Advantage: Static compliance is a relic. In a dynamic regulatory landscape, agility is your best friend. Establish a flexible compliance framework that can adapt to changes swiftly. Train your team to embrace change, making compliance an integral part of your organizational culture.

Collaboration Across Silos: Break down departmental silos. Collaboration ensures that compliance is not just a legal obligation but a collective responsibility. Foster open communication channels where different departments share insights and challenges. A united front is a resilient one.

### Advocacy: Shaping Policy, Shaping Destiny

- Beyond Compliance: Advocacy as a Strategic Lever: Don't just react; be a proactive force in shaping policy. Engage in advocacy efforts to influence regulations in your favor. Establish relationships with policymakers, contribute to public consultations, and participate in industry associations. When you shape policy, you shape your business destiny.

- The Power of a Unified Voice: Advocacy is not a solo act. Join forces with like-minded businesses and industry associations. A unified voice carries more weight and can influence policy decisions. It's not just about compliance; it's about actively participating in the creation of the rules.

Regularly update your team on regulatory developments. Invest in training programs to enhance their understanding of evolving regulations. An informed team is a compliant team.

Expect challenges. Whether it's sudden regulatory shifts or internal resistance to change, have contingency plans in place. Embrace a mindset of continuous improvement, learning from setbacks to strengthen your approach.

As we navigate the intricacies of adapting to changing regulations, remember: this is not a passive strategic endeavor. It's an active strategy that positions your business at the forefront of success. Anticipate, adapt, and advocate—these are the pillars of resilience in an ever-evolving regulatory landscape. Your compliance path is not just about following rules; it's about leading the way into a future you help shape.

In this dynamic dance with regulations, the steps you take today will define the rhythm of your success tomorrow. It's not just about compliance; it's about conquering the regulatory maze and emerging victorious on the other side. Embrace a new era, where compliance is not a burden but a strategic advantage.

# Chapter 12
# Conclusion

As we reach the end of "Lend & Earn," it becomes evident that the landscape of lending and earning is not merely a domain of numbers and transactions, but a realm where financial aspirations and realities intersect. This book has not only been about imparting knowledge; it has served as a guide in your financial development, a testament to the power of informed decision-making in the world of lending.

Reflecting on the path traversed, we recognize that the evolution of lending practices is not just a chronicle of the past, but a reflection of our own growth. From understanding key market trends to mastering the role of technology, each chapter has laid a foundation for a stronger financial understanding. As you've absorbed these chapters, you've been equipped with the tools to assess your financial readiness, align your lending goals with broader financial objectives, and choose the right platform that caters to your needs.

Risk, often perceived as a daunting concept, has been redefined in these pages. It's about more than balancing risk and return; it's understanding the psychology behind it. Through strategies for risk mitigation and profiling, you've gained insights to transform uncertainty into a strategic asset.

Delving deeper, we've explored the human aspect of lending - understanding and leveraging borrower profiles. It's about looking beyond mere numbers, understanding borrower needs, and forging relationships based on trust and effective communication. The focus on legal and ethical considerations has underscored the importance of responsible lending, ensuring that your practices are not only profitable but also sustainable.

The digital revolution in lending has unveiled new horizons. From fintech innovations to the role of AI and big data, technology has been presented as a catalyst for efficiency and enhanced borrower experience. And as you've explored these technological advancements, you've been part of a movement reshaping the lending landscape.

Growing your lending business isn't just about expansion; it's about cultivating a mindset geared towards growth, balancing ambition with stability. The strategies outlined in these chapters have paved a roadmap for sustainable growth, emphasizing the importance of marketing, brand building, and the power of partnerships.

Incorporating lending into personal finance has been another crucial aspect of this book. Lending, when thoughtfully integrated into your financial plan, can serve as a robust investment tool, complementing traditional investments and balancing your overall portfolio.

Our global exploration of international lending markets has highlighted the unique opportunities and challenges of cross-border lending. Understanding cultural nuances, navigating regulatory environments, and managing risks specific to international lending have been key elements of this exploration.

Finally, looking towards the future, we've ventured into predicting emerging trends and exploring innovative lending models. The future of lending is dynamic, and staying ahead means being adaptable, proactive, and informed.

As we close this final chapter, remember that "Lend & Earn" is more than just a book; it's a manifesto for financial empowerment. It's about taking control of your financial destiny, using the knowledge and tools acquired to make informed decisions, and seizing the opportunities that come your way. The principles and strategies detailed here are not just theoretical concepts; they're practical, actionable, and designed to resonate with your financial aspirations.

Thank you for embarking on this enlightening path with "Lend & Earn." As you turn the last page, carry with you not just the knowledge but the confidence to navigate the ever-evolving world of lending and earning. Here's to your success, both in the insights from this book and in the vast, exciting world of financial opportunities.